BEING HEUMANN

BEING HEUMANN

AN
UNREPENTANT MEMOIR
OF A
DISABILITY RIGHTS
ACTIVIST

JUDITH HEUMANN

WITH KRISTEN JOINER

BEACON PRESS
BOSTON

BEACON PRESS
Boston, Massachusetts
www.beacon.org

Beacon Press books
are published under the auspices of
the Unitarian Universalist Association of Congregations.

23 22 21 20   8 7 6 5 4 3 2 1

This book is printed on acid-free paper that meets the uncoated paper
ANSI/NISO specifications for permanence as revised in 1992.

Text design and composition by Kim Arney

Library of Congress Cataloging-in-Publication Data

Names: Heumann, Judith E., author. | Beacon Press.
Title: Being Heumann : an unrepentant memoir of a disability rights
activist / Judith Heumann, with Kristen Joiner.
Description: Boston : Beacon Press, [2019] |
Includes bibliographical references and index.
Identifiers: LCCN 2019026271 (print) | LCCN 2019026272 (ebook) |
ISBN 9780807019290 (Hardcover : acid-free paper) |
ISBN 9780807019382 (ebook)
Subjects: LCSH: Heumann, Judith E. | Human rights workers—United
States—Biography. | People with disabilities—United States—
Biography. | Teachers—United States—Biography.
Classification: LCC JC571 .H49 2019 (print) | LCC JC571 (ebook) |
DDC 362.4092 [B]—dc23
LC record available at https://lccn.loc.gov/2019026271
LC ebook record available at https://lccn.loc.gov/2019026272

JUDITH

To my mother and father,
Ilse and Werner Heumann, of blessed memory,
for the belief that I could do anything.

To Marca Bristo, a fellow fighter
who shared a vision of how the world should be.

KRISTEN

To my mother and father,
Laurel Warnick Joiner and Brian Joiner,
who showed me what it means
to truly live by your values.

CONTENTS

A Note from Judy ix
Prologue xi

PART ONE BROOKLYN, NEW YORK, 1953
CHAPTER 1 The Butterfly 3
CHAPTER 2 Insubordinate 28
CHAPTER 3 To Fight or Not to Fight 52
CHAPTER 4 Fear of Flying 65

PART TWO BERKELEY, CALIFORNIA, 1977
CHAPTER 5 Detained 85
CHAPTER 6 Occupation Army 98
CHAPTER 7 Soldiers in Combat 119
CHAPTER 8 The White House 131

PART THREE BERKELEY, CALIFORNIA, 1981
CHAPTER 9 The Reckoning 151
CHAPTER 10 Chingona 172
CHAPTER 11 Humans 184
CHAPTER 12 Our Story 201

Acknowledgments 212
Notes 217

A NOTE FROM JUDY

FOR A LONG TIME I resisted the idea of writing my story. Not because I was afraid of revisiting these memories, although it has been difficult at times, I admit. But rather because I have never felt like it was my story alone to tell. Everything I've done in my life, I never would have been able to do alone—whether it was my mother and father or my brothers, my friends from school, or my fellow activists helping, listening, laughing, and leading. I have felt their love and support whispering in my ear throughout this entire process, and I hope my story allows them to shine in the way I remember them. At times I have changed the names of people and certain details for the sake of privacy and recreated some situations based on my memory and the memory of those around me.

And so, with that caveat, I share with you my story.

Thank you for listening.

PROLOGUE

I NEVER WISHED I didn't have a disability.

I'm fairly certain my parents didn't either. I never asked them, but if I had, I don't think they would have said that our lives would have been better if I hadn't had a disability. They accepted it and moved forward. That was who they were. That was their way. They deliberately decided not to tell me what the doctor had advised when I recovered from polio and it became clear I was never going to walk again. It wasn't until I was in my thirties that I discovered what he'd suggested.

"I recommend that you place her in an institution," he said.

It wasn't personal. It didn't have anything to do with our family being German immigrants. Nor was it ill intentioned. I am sure he sincerely believed that the very best thing for these young parents to do would be to have their two-year-old child raised in an institution.

In many ways, institutionalization was the status quo in 1949. Parents weren't necessarily even encouraged to visit their institutionalized children. Kids with disabilities were considered a hardship, economically and socially. They brought stigma to the family. People thought that when someone in your family had a disability it was because someone had done something wrong.

I DON'T KNOW how my parents responded to the doctor, because my family didn't talk a lot about things like this. But I am sure my parents would have found the idea of putting me in an institution very disturbing. Both my mother and my father had been made orphans by the Holocaust. As teenagers they'd been sent to the United States. It was the time when Hitler was coming into power, when things were getting bad enough that people worried about the safety of their children but didn't think it was going to get as bad as it did. My father came to live with an uncle in Brooklyn at fourteen, and he was lucky that his three brothers followed very soon after. My mother was an only child and was sent alone to live in Chicago with someone she didn't know at all. The story was that a distant relative came from the States to visit my mother's family in Germany and brought news of the worsening situation. The information convinced my grandparents to send my mother, their one child, away to live with this distant relative.

I have often imagined what it must have felt like for my mother. You're twelve years old and one day someone you don't know, someone you've never met before, comes to visit your family and two weeks later you're suddenly gone from Germany forever, living alone in Chicago with unfamiliar people. My mother always thought that her family would be together again. Even during the war, she was working to save money to bring her parents over. Only later did she learn that they'd been killed.

IF I'D BEEN born just ten years earlier and become disabled in Germany, it is almost certain that the German doctor would also have advised that I be institutionalized. The difference is that instead of growing up being fed by nurses in a small room with white walls and a roommate, I would have been taken to a special clinic, and at that special clinic, I would have been killed.

Before Auschwitz and Dachau, there were institutions where disabled children were eliminated. Hitler's pilot project for what would ultimately become mass genocide started with disabled children. Doctors encouraged the parents to hand their young children over to specially designated pediatric clinics, where they were either intentionally starved or given a lethal injection. When the program expanded to include older children, the doctors experimented with gassing.

Five thousand children were murdered in these institutions.

The Nazis considered people with disabilities a genetic and financial burden on society. Life unworthy of life.

So when an authority figure in their new country, a doctor, said to my parents, "We will take your daughter out of your home and raise her," they never would have agreed to it. They came from a country where families got separated, some children sent away, others taken from their families by the authorities and never returned—all as part of a campaign of systematic dehumanization and murder.

Their daughter, disabled or not, wasn't going anywhere.

MY PARENTS WEREN'T obstinate or antiauthoritarian; they were thinkers. They had learned what happens when hatred and inhumanity are accepted. Both my father and my mother were brave people who lived by their values. They had personally experienced what happens when an entire country chooses not to see something simply because it is not what they wish to see. As a result, they never accepted anything at face value. When something doesn't feel right, they taught us, you must question it— whether it is an instruction from an authority or what a teacher says in class. At the same time, my parents didn't dwell on the past or on things that were done to them.

They didn't *forget* the past, and they definitely learned from it, but Ilse and Werner Heumann moved forward. Especially Ilse.

She was an optimist. And a fighter.

And so am I.

I can't say I was thinking about all these things when we took over the San Francisco Federal Building, or even when I took on the New York City Board of Education. Only now, looking back, can I see how it all came together to turn me into the person I was to become.

PART ONE

BROOKLYN, NEW YORK

1953

CHAPTER 1

THE BUTTERFLY

SOME PEOPLE SAY that what I did changed the world. But really, I simply refused to accept what I was told about who I could be. And I was willing to make a fuss about it.

I must say right up front, though, that it wasn't actually an "I," it was a "we." For any story of changing the world is always the story of many. Many ideas, many arguments; many discussions; many late-night, punchy, falling-apart-laughing brainstorms; many believers; many friendships; many failures; many times of almost giving up; and many, many, *many* people. This is my story, yes, but I was one in a multitude, and I hope I will do justice to the many heroes, those who are alive and those no longer among us.

To begin at the beginning, I will tell you about what happened after my parents refused to institutionalize me, about my childhood. So you will understand what the world was like then—before we took over the San Francisco Federal Building, before people crawled up the steps of the Capitol, before systemic change began.

In 1953 I was six. Dwight D. Eisenhower was president, Elizabeth Taylor was a box-office star, Jackie Robinson had just recently broken the color line in baseball, and World War II had ended a mere eight years earlier. Elvis Presley had three years to go before his breakthrough on *The Ed Sullivan Show*, the Dodgers were still in Brooklyn, and much of America, celebrating the advent of peace and prosperity, was in the throes of having seven million babies—the baby boom. Less obvious than the general sense of prosperity was the discontent that simmered below the surface among the people living lives segregated from the wealth of post–World War II America, whether African Americans, Latinos, or other minorities. In 1953 the National Association for the Advancement of Colored People was in the midst of taking its class-action suit, *Brown v. Board of Education of Topeka*, to the Supreme Court; two years later Rosa Parks would refuse to give up her seat to a white passenger on a Montgomery, Alabama, bus.

To my parents, the events of their new country were of great interest, and they, along with all the other immigrants of our Brooklyn neighborhood, followed the news closely. I, on the other hand, at six, understood very little of the national news, but from my six-year-old perspective, I could have told you a great deal about what life was like for someone like me. One of the nearly forty-three thousand American children affected by the 1949 polio epidemic, I was a quadriplegic. Though my life wasn't marked with the little "Whites Only" signs that signaled segregation in the South, the life I lived was also a segregated one. Of course I didn't understand this for a long time, shielded as I was by the love of my family and friends. For me, at six, my city block was my whole world, and there was no place I would rather have been.

In the summer of 1953, you would have quite likely found me on my way to Arlene's house, next door, pushing myself in my manual wheelchair down the sidewalk in tiny increments. To get to Arlene's, my journey started with my mother pushing me down the ramp from our house to the sidewalk. Once there, I would grip the rims of my wheelchair tires and inch my way along. It would be another fifteen years before I would have an electric wheelchair. At that time a Canadian, George Klein, motivated by the needs of returning World War II veterans, was in the process of inventing the electric wheelchair, but the chair was still four years away from mass production.

Because my bout with polio as an infant had left me with very little strength in my arms, moving my manual wheelchair took all my effort. The key to getting to Arlene's and back was a minuscule incline in the sidewalk between our two houses. It was the tiniest incline you can imagine and it would have been invisible to any pedestrian walking by, but I knew that if I could get myself to the top of it I could then coast down the other side. As I worked my way up the sidewalk, I could hear the radio through our kitchen window, where my little four-year-old brother, Joey, was eating his cereal with my mother and my baby brother, Ricky, my father having left for our butcher shop in the wee hours of the morning.

Nearly at the top of the incline, I held my breath as my chair crept up the last infinitesimal rise, the sun hot on the back of my head, hair falling over my eyes. Without thinking, I took one hand off the wheel to brush the hair off my face. The wheel, without the stabilizing force of both my hands, slipped, and I rolled all the way back to my original spot. Sighing, I lifted my head and looked around hopefully. Any kids out yet? I looked for anyone who might be able to give me a little push. But the street was quiet. I took a deep breath, bent my head, and started over.

Sometime later—five minutes? ten? thirty? . . . time has a different meaning when you're six—I landed in front of Arlene's stoop and looked at the three steps up to the door. This was the part of the expedition that made me feel awkward. I couldn't get my wheelchair up the steps to ring Arlene's doorbell, which meant I had to sit on the sidewalk in front of her house and yell for her to come out and play.

I sat for a few minutes. Arlene's house had a narrow, red-brick front with white siding on the upper level and a small patch of flowers on a small rectangular lawn. It was just like ours, minus our blue hydrangeas. If the car was in front of the house, I knew the Almskogs were home—with any luck, someone would come out and see me. I shifted my gaze to our house. I could hear Uncle Frank, who wasn't our uncle but we called him uncle anyway, yelling from the Voehls' house on the other side of Arlene's, but no one came out of the Voehls' house either. Eyeing Arlene's bedroom window on the second floor, I watched for her shadow. Her white curtains stirred gently in the wind. I glanced up and down the street one last time, to see if anyone had come out to play. A bird chirped, flew across the empty street, and landed on the Voehls' roof.

Gathering my courage, I called out, "Arleeene, can you come out and play!" I waited, embarrassed. I had to yell loud enough that Arlene or her mom or dad or brothers would hear me, but didn't want to yell so loud that the whole block could hear me.

Nothing. I couldn't hear anyone inside the house.

I tried again and yelled a bit louder.

"Arlene, can you come out and play?" I paused and watched the house.

Still nothing.

I stopped worrying about whether or not the whole block could hear me and hollered.

"Arlene!" I shouted, as loudly as I could. "Come out and play!!"

"Hi, Judy!" Arlene's mom came to the door. "Arlene will be out in a minute."

Five minutes later Arlene appeared at the front door in a green-checkered dress, her brown hair down, a doll tucked under her arm. My mom and Arlene's mom, whom we called Aunt Ivy, always made us wear dresses. So did our best friend Mary's mom, whom we called Aunt Ruth.

Arlene leaped down the three steps.

"What should we do?"

"Let's see if Mary can play," I said. Arlene pushed my wheel-chair the three seconds it took to get to Mary's house and then went up the steps and rang the doorbell to see if Mary could play. Aunt Ruth said yes and Mary came right out, her blond hair tied in a ponytail, a doll in hand, and she and Arlene pushed me into my backyard so we could play dolls in the shade of our big maple tree, which we loved to do. I was lucky that Mary and Arlene lived on my side of the street because I never could have gotten my chair off my sidewalk, across the street, and up the curb on the other side, no matter how many inclines there were in be-tween. For me, a curb was the Great Wall of China.

Eventually, other children on the block would come out to play. Patsy, Beth, Teddy, my brother Joey, Mary's brothers Eddie and Billy, Arlene's brother Paul, and Frankie, who was older. The street was one way and few cars drove on it.

It didn't occur to me then to think it unusual that I joined in all the kids' games in my wheelchair. Because there was never a question of whether or not I would play, too—we all figured out a way for me to do whatever everyone was doing. Even when we jumped rope or roller-skated, we figured it out. We'd put roller skates over my shoes and I would pretend to be skating in my chair, or I'd turn the rope for the jumpers, or play in some other way. I didn't know anything different. Now I know that this was the way it was because we were kids, and kids are problem solvers. But it taught me, at a very early age, that most things are possible when you assume problems can be solved.

On Saturday nights the parents were home and often outside, the dads barbecuing and the moms chatting, setting the picnic table. We would smell the hamburgers and frankfurters on the grills and wait hungrily for them to be ready, playing in the street. On Sundays, Joey and I went to Hebrew school. Afterward, we'd pile into the car and go to the beach to visit my uncle Leon, or Uncle Alfred and the cousins in Seagate, a neighborhood in Coney Island, or swim in our inflatable backyard pool.

Then, in September, summer ended and school started. The mornings became chilly and everything changed. September was when Mary and her siblings went to Catholic school, and Arlene, her brothers, and my little brother Joey went to public school—and I should have been going with them, but I wasn't.

I still remember the day I was five and my mother had taken me to register for kindergarten. My mother helped me put on a nice dress, pushed me to school, and pulled my wheelchair up the steps. But the principal refused to allow me to enter.

"Judy is a fire hazard," he said, explaining to my shocked mother how the school system saw wheelchairs as a dangerous obstruction. Children who used wheelchairs were not permitted to attend school. I would stay home.

And so had begun, from that day forward, my mother's long fight to get me into school. It wasn't that my father wasn't involved. He cared very much about my education, but he was working at our butcher shop from four in the morning until seven at night. The day-to-day work of fighting fell on my mother, which I take as a sign. Because if the universe really hadn't wanted me to go to school, it wouldn't have made Ilse Heumann my mother. Telling Ilse Heumann that something wasn't possible was a big mistake.

One of the first things my mother did was try to get me into a local yeshiva, a Jewish day school. The principal at the yeshiva had told my mother I could go to school if I learned enough Hebrew, no doubt trying to get rid of her politely. I honestly don't think my mother realized that this was his way of saying no. Probably because my mother didn't really hear the word "no." She listened for the smallest crack in any negative answer that would turn it into a yes. My mother was the embodiment of persistence.

Which is funny, because she was so easy to underestimate from the outside. My father called her Mighty Mite. Not much over five feet tall, she had a big beautiful smile that put people at ease. You didn't really see the steel underneath until it blindsided you.

So, whether she thought it was reasonable or not, my mother was going to make sure I learned Hebrew. She asked my physical therapist's wife, who was Israeli, to teach me Hebrew, and for weeks, my mother drove me to their apartment every day for tutoring. Until, as my mother joked later, I spoke Hebrew better than the students. But when she called the principal to tell him that I'd learned Hebrew and she wanted to enroll me at the end of the summer, the principal, likely shocked that my mother had actually followed through, backtracked.

"Well, it's just not going to work," he said.

My mother did not cry over spilled milk. She moved on.

Not long after the yeshiva turned us down, the New York City Board of Education called my mother to tell her about a possible program for me, and invited us to come and visit. This was the first time that my mother realized that there was no expectation that I would attend an integrated school with nondisabled children. When we visited the program, I remember thinking that it didn't seem like the school my friends told me about—kids were not at their desks and it seemed chaotic. My mother and father refused to put me into this program.

A few weeks into what would have been my first-grade year, the Board of Education called my mother and told her I was now eligible for home instruction. Whereupon they sent a teacher, Mrs. Campfield, to our house two days a week—the first day for an hour; and the second day for an hour and a half—to sit at the card table in my bedroom and teach me. The idea that I could learn anything meaningful in two and a half hours of instruction a week was, of course, ludicrous, although Mrs. Campfield was a nice woman and I did like having someone other than my mother teaching me. My parents weren't given instruction materials or books or anything to supplement my instruction. Obviously, there was no intention that home instruction was to be comparable in any way to what Joey or my friends were receiving.

But I had no idea of any of this because I was just a kid.

And I was a happy kid. As far as I knew, the Catholic kids on my block went to Catholic school, the Protestant kids and my brother went to public school, and I went to "school" at home; we all went to "different" schools. When Joey started kindergarten that year, in 1953, and I stayed at home I'd had a vague feeling that something was not quite right, but I couldn't have put it into words.

At home, I did the meager homework that Mrs. Campfield left for me, but what I mainly did was read. I read and read and read. In the afternoon, when my brother came home from school or a friend came over, I would know it was time to go out and play. Then I'd play until it was time for my afternoon extracurricular activity for that day. After the regular school day I participated in all the same extracurricular activities as Joey and my cousins and friends. I had Hebrew school on Sundays, Mondays, and Thursdays, Scouts on Tuesdays, and piano on Wednesdays. In my afternoon activities I never felt different from the other kids, even though I was the only one in a wheelchair. Well, I did sometimes feel a little awkward about getting schlepped up the stairs backwards to Brownies, or getting carried down the back steps and through the garbage behind the synagogue to get to the elevator for Hebrew classes. One day my poor mother tripped on a broom as she was tipping my wheelchair back, bouncing it down the steps, and I flipped out of my wheelchair and busted my lip. But other than wondering why they didn't just have a ramp like the one we had at home, I didn't think much about it. Once I got to where I was going I was always perfectly content to do my arts and crafts or study Hebrew and learn about Jewish culture with all the other kids.

And so, in the humidity of summer I played in the streets until September, when everyone went to school and I stayed home. Then Mrs. Campfield would knock on our door, worksheets in hand, and Hebrew school, piano lessons, and Brownies started. The leaves changed colors and dropped, and the snow came, blanketing our street. Aunt Ruth, Aunt Ivy, and our neighbor Mrs. Malam—a scout leader and later my math tutor—would come for coffee with my mother. After "school" with Mrs. Campfield I played outside with Arlene, Mary, Patsy, Beth, and Teddy. On the Jewish holidays we went to synagogue. On Sundays we went to Hebrew school, and afterward we'd visit aunts, uncles, and cousins, or we'd go to museums.

Other times my parents would buy tickets for the theater or ballet or the opera. From his youth, my father had always loved these activities, sometimes walking miles to get to the theater in his neighboring town in Germany, where he would hand out fliers just so he could get into the performances. He made sure we were exposed to arts and culture. None of the buses or trains were accessible, but my mother or father would fold my wheelchair and put it into the trunk of our car, and off we would go.

On certain Sundays, we'd eat a lovely brunch of bagels, lox, and whitefish, with delicious sweets, eggs, and pastrami, cooked with care by my dad. The company at our dining-room table was never boring. My father liked to provoke discussion and create debates. At that time, we had morning and evening newspapers, and he, my mother, and my brothers and I would read newspapers, magazines, and books all the time. In our house, if you held an opinion on something, you had to be prepared to defend it. We argued, discussed, and laughed so much that I am sure the neighbors could hear us through the windows. Then, when summer came and school ended, it would be time to start playing in the streets again.

In this way, Ricky grew and started walking, Joey started first grade and then second, and I turned seven and eight.

If I were painting those days in color, I would use bright pinks and lavenders. There were curbs and steps to conquer, and I wasn't allowed in school, but I was a cheerful, contented girl.

Until the day we walked to the candy store.

I THINK IT WAS A BEAUTIFUL SUNNY DAY, but it might have been cloudy. I don't remember. What I do remember was being caught up in my conversation with Arlene as she pushed me in my wheelchair, talking about what we were going to buy at the candy store, or what we wanted to do later that day. We were pleased to be walking around the corner to buy sweets. In front of Dr. Nagler's brick house, which I knew was Dr. Nagler's house because I'd been there with my mother for her doctor appointments, we paused to cross the street. Arlene turned me around to lower my wheelchair off the curb, pushed me across the street, and then, once we reached the other side, she put her foot on the metal bar on the back of my chair, tipped me and the chair back, and lifted my chair onto the sidewalk. As we did this, a few kids came toward us from the opposite direction. They were walking slowly down the sidewalk. As they passed, Arlene shifted my wheelchair to the side to make room for them. We didn't know them and didn't pay much attention, engrossed as we were in our conversation. So I was surprised when one of the kids turned suddenly to look at me.

He stood in front of me, staring down at me in my wheelchair.

"Are you sick?" he asked me loudly.

I stared at him, not understanding.

"What?"

"Are you sick?" he repeated, insistently.

His voice boomed. I shook my head, trying to clear the words away. I was still confused but couldn't speak.

"Are. You. Sick?" he asked, slowing the words down as if I were a toddler.

The world went silent as the words reverberated in my head. I couldn't hear anything except those words.

"Are. You. Sick. Sick . . . Sick . . . Sick . . . Sick?"

I shrank down, frozen with confusion, wanting to cover myself up with something. Anything to hide from that question, the boy's insistent eyes on me.

"Are you sick?" he asked insistently, almost shouting.

Suddenly I became aware of Dr. Nagler's house behind me, and my face turned a cringingly deep red.

Does he think I'm going to the doctor? But he's not *my* doctor, I thought, fiercely. I fought back tears. I couldn't, *wouldn't*, cry in front of everyone. I *wasn't* sick. It made no sense. I knew I wasn't. But then, why was he asking me that?

I became uncertain of myself. *Was* I sick?

I saw myself through his eyes, and the light around me shifted. Shadows emerged from the corners of my mind; previously submerged words, thoughts, and half-heard conversations tumbled into the glare of a spotlight.

In a blinding flash, everything in my life made a perverse kind of sense.

I couldn't go to this school, I couldn't go to that school. I couldn't do this, I couldn't do that, I couldn't walk up the stairs, I couldn't open doors, I couldn't even cross the street.

I *was* different. But I'd always known that. It wasn't that.

It was the world and how it saw me.

The world thought I was sick.

Sick people stayed home in bed. They didn't go out to play, or go to school. They weren't expected to go outside, to be a part of things, to be a part of the world.

I wasn't expected to be a part of the world.

Abruptly, I knew this to be true. As if the knowledge had already existed for years throughout my entire body. I felt nauseatingly humiliated at the idea that everyone else had known this but me. Had they kept it from me? The embarrassment settled in as a cold ball deep in my stomach, where I could feel it spreading into my limbs.

Was it sunny or cloudy? I don't know. I remember Arlene was pushing me, we were going to the store to buy candy, and we were chatting.

And I was a butterfly, becoming a caterpillar.

That night I said nothing to my family. At dinner, as my brothers loudly discussed something with my parents, I was quiet. I ate and then went to bed. The next morning, I woke up, had breakfast, and went out to play. With Mary and Arlene, Patsy and Beth, Teddy and all the kids on the block, I played jump rope. Then I sat with them and talked about all the same things we normally talked about. On Monday, my brother went to school, Mrs. Campfield came, my brother came home and we went to Hebrew school. Then on Thursday I had piano and Brownies. It was all the same, but something was different. I was self-conscious now of feeling changed in some unspeakable way I didn't fully understand. After that day, nothing was ever quite the same.

Around that time I became conscious of the faulty logic behind my not being allowed to go to school with my brother. The school had steps, yes, but my father carried me up two flights of steps all the time to get to services at synagogue. Why couldn't I just be carried up the steps to school every day? I didn't get it. It seemed like such a simple problem, the kind of problem we solved every day on my block. Although I knew my parents wanted me in school, they didn't really talk about the *reasoning* behind why the school district objected. And I didn't ask. Perhaps because it felt like a topic so shaded and veiled that I kept quiet about it too.

Then, not long after the incident on the way to the candy store, my mother finally succeeded at getting me into a school.

And everything changed.

ON MY FIRST DAY OF SCHOOL, I woke up early. My father had kissed me good luck before he went to work, sometime between four and five in the morning. After he left I couldn't fall back asleep. School! My heart thumped with anxiety and excitement.

Lying in bed, restless, I shifted my arms and looked toward the accordion door between my bedroom and the kitchen. I wished my mother would come walking in to get me dressed; I didn't think I could wait for the bus to come at seven. But the house remained utterly quiet. Sinking back into my pillow I stared at the ceiling and took a breath. Maybe I could will her to come. Turning toward the door, I closed my eyes and concentrated with all my might, picturing my mother coming into the bedroom. I opened my eyes hopefully. Still nothing. Giving up, I lay back down and closed my eyes. I was used to waiting.

Over the three years since we'd been turned down by the yeshiva, my mother had been searching for alternatives and organizing with other parents. We didn't have a lot of money, so any potential solution for me had to be either a public option or something that fit our family's slim budget. My mother had sought out parents of other kids who had had polio, researched schools, met with people from the New York City Board of Education, talked to whoever would talk to her, and ferreted out information. Because of this I'd been placed on a waiting list for Health Conservation 21, a program for kids with disabilities that was offered in various schools around the district. Eventually I'd reached the top of the waiting list, had been asked to come for an assessment, and then finally had been invited to a class. Being put on a waiting list and evaluated for my ability to attend a public school in the United States should have been illegal, but that was overlooked by the Board of Education. And, since the screening hadn't initiated until late fall it was winter by the time I got approved, which meant that I was starting school halfway through the fourth grade. I was nine years old.

My mother wanted me to wear the pink dress with the flowers for my first day of school. Since I was reliant on my mother's help to get up and get dressed, as well as for the rest of my daily necessities, this put me at a disadvantage when I wanted to wear something different than what she wanted. Normally she would have just picked something, taken it out of my closet, and gotten me dressed, anxious to get my brother up and going, but this time she took the time to let me choose and I got to wear what I wanted instead. I picked my green dress.

First, my mother put my blue tights on, then she put my feet into my shoes and hooked the shoes into my long leg braces with the spinal corset. Then she stood me up, put my dress on, and gave me my crutches so I could slowly walk to the bathroom, which was immediately to the right of my bedroom. At that time I still had enough strength in my arms to go to the bathroom by myself. My mother then helped me brush my long brown hair to make it shine. I got into my wheelchair and pushed myself to the dining room, while my mother ran upstairs to make sure Joey was awake. Sitting by myself at the table, I ate a spoonful of cereal, half listening to the radio talk about the snow.

I was finally going to start to learn in a classroom with kids my age. Better late than never, I thought. I poked at the corn flakes in my bowl. What would it be like to go to school? My stomach somersaulted with anticipation at the thought. Leaving home for school was a massive change. I'd been hearing about classes and grades from my brother and my friends for years, but I'd never actually been in a classroom nor even been told what grade I was in—and now I knew. I was going to be in fourth grade, although at an entirely new school.

No one I knew would be going to Health Conservation 21, since the program was only for disabled kids, although I didn't really know what this meant. While I had casually met some disabled kids in the hospital, I had never spent long periods of time with them. I thought about this fact, nibbling at a tiny bite of cereal. I was nervous about taking the bus by myself. I had never been on a bus. I wondered how I would get onto it, since all the buses I knew of had steps. I was also confused about how long I should expect to be on the bus. My mother had told me the bus was supposed to come to our house at around 7:00 a.m. and that we were supposed to arrive at school at around 8:30 a.m. But if those times were right, it would mean that I'd be on the bus for an hour and a half, which seemed weird to me because the school was only fifteen minutes away by car.

Giving up on my breakfast, I put my spoon down.

"Mommm! I'm done!" I yelled impatiently. I wanted to pack my school bag with a pencil holder and a notebook.

My mother went to the front of the house to look out the window for the bus. But it was Lucky, my German shepherd, who heard it first and started barking. As the bus turned onto our street, my mother pushed me out the kitchen door and down the ramp, and then through the gate. I tried to help by pushing my wheelchair, my hands on the metal rim of the wheels, but it was cold and my coat got in the way. Once we got to the alley, she went to the driveway outside our neighbor's house and pushed me down the driveway to the street where the bus was waiting. The sky was streaked with pink and orange as my mother and I waited for the bus driver and his assistant, whom I would soon learn to call Lois, to lower the wheelchair lift.

From where I sat, I could see a face peeking out the bus window, looking down at me. My mother stood to the side as the driver shifted my chair onto the lift, while Lois, from inside the bus, pushed the buttons that slowly lifted me into the bus. My mother gave me a quick kiss and then, once I was on the bus, waved.

"Have a good day, honey!" She called. "I'll be here waiting for you after school." I knew that also meant that Lucky would be home, which was a comforting thought. The bus driver then closed the doors and walked to the front to get back into the bus, while Lois hooked my wheelchair to keep it from moving and put a seatbelt on me.

Now I was really excited. I was on a wheelchair-accessible bus!

As the bus slowly lurched into motion, Lois explained to me that we would be picking up other students before we arrived at school. She and the driver were both very friendly.

Surreptitiously I surveyed my surroundings. The bus was regular size and had space for six wheelchairs. I was the second student on the bus. The other student, a girl who was also in a wheelchair, looked at me and smiled, but not much was said. Normally outgoing, suddenly I was shy. We picked up a number of other students, some of whom were also in wheelchairs. An hour and a half, and I don't know how many stops, later, the bus pulled up to a massive red-brick building. Over the front door was written "P.S. 219," which I knew stood for "Public School 219." Four stories high, the school took up an entire block. There were a few other wheelchair-accessible buses arriving at the same time.

Outside the building, I saw kids everywhere, walking down the street, sitting on the steps, standing in twos and threes on the corner, coming from every direction. This is my school! I thought happily. As I watched the other students, a bell rang and the kids outside the school began pouring through big wide-open doors in the front of the building.

A few adults stood by, waiting for our bus and a few other wheelchair-accessible buses to park. These were people, I later learned, who would assist us with getting in and out of school, going to the bathroom, and getting to various therapy appointments. I watched the process, fascinated, as one kid after another got off the bus, either walking down the steps with their braces and crutches or going down the lift and being taken into the school. Finally it was my turn. One of the adults who had been waiting for us asked my name, introduced herself, and then wheeled me to my classroom.

Another woman met us at the classroom door.

"You must be Judy." She smiled. "I am Mrs. Parker. I'll be your teacher." Mrs. Parker asked me to sit at a desk for two with a girl she introduced as Shelley, who happened to be one of the girls I'd seen on my bus. Shelley also used a wheelchair and, I learned, had had polio. The class had only eight or nine students in it, and every single kid was in a wheelchair or wore a brace or both. They seemed to be all different ages, which confused me. This was fourth grade? I'd never been in school before, but I knew that grades meant you were a certain age. Joey had started kindergarten when he was five, first grade when he was six, and second grade when he was seven. The curly-haired boy in the wheelchair next to me looked about my age, but I was sure that the tall girl with the brown ponytail in the corner had to be at least sixteen or seventeen.

I was relieved that the work was easy. Mrs. Parker spoke very slowly, and the worksheets she handed out repeated much of what I'd done with Mrs. Campfield. I'd been worried about how hard things would be, but I finished my work quickly. Around me other kids were still working. I noticed that some seemed to be getting pulled out of class at random times.

"Therapy," Shelley whispered to me, when I asked her where they were going. They were getting physical therapy, occupational therapy, or speech therapy.

I was reading a book while some of the other pupils finished one of the worksheets when Mrs. Parker told us to put our books away for lunch. We moved to another room and sat around small tables. Eating my sandwich, I quietly listened to the kids talking around me. People sounded friendly, and occasionally someone asked me a question. I still felt very shy. I could hear the footsteps of kids thumping above us and their calls when they played outside, but I didn't see any of these kids. I was curious about them.

After about an hour for lunch, I was surprised when Mrs. Parker turned out the lights and announced that it was time for our rest hour. I hadn't napped since I was four, but I followed the lead of the other students and tried to sit quietly in my wheelchair with my eyes closed. I was happy when Mrs. Parker finally turned the lights back on and handed out another worksheet. I quickly completed it and then went back to reading again.

It seemed like no time at all had gone by when Mrs. Parker snapped her book closed and asked us to start packing our things up to go home.

This was my first day of school.

In the days that followed, I started to feel more comfortable and rapidly made friends with the other children in the class who had many different types of disabilities. A number of students who had cerebral palsy needed some help with eating their lunch, which staff helped them with, but I discovered it was fun to help a few of my friends also. I loved feeling useful. I began to listen for the finer details of people's preferences. How did someone wish to eat? How quickly did they chew and want help with the next bite of food? Did they want their potato chips before, during, or after their sandwich? It turned out that Joanie LaPadula, the tall girl in the corner with the ponytail, who was older, as I'd thought, didn't know how to read very well. Neither did another older girl, Jill Kirschner. I started helping them improve their reading.

We all had fun and laughed a lot. Although some of my new friends didn't speak as clearly as others, it never occurred to me not to take the time to listen, because they were my friends.

I soon learned more about the "kids upstairs," which is what we called the nondisabled kids who went to school above us. The kids upstairs were different from us. They were the regular kids who went to school at P.S. 219. We were the special-education kids, who were in Health Conservation 21, in the basement. We were kept completely separate, and although I didn't know it then, our days were totally different.

First of all, the kids upstairs were in school much longer than we were. They were taught a regulated curriculum that required them to be in school from eight-thirty in the morning until three in the afternoon—about six hours of instruction. The quantity and quality of their instruction was designed to ensure that they would progress in school, from elementary school to middle school, and then to high school and, ideally, college. In addition, school for the kids upstairs was mandatory. School is how we pass knowledge, skills, and values on to children—for the good of society. In America, school is considered so important, that, since 1918, it has been compulsory.

For everyone except us.

Nobody, not the teachers, not the principal, not the New York City Board of Education, expected the special-ed kids to learn. Many didn't expect us to progress from elementary school, to middle school, high school, university. We were expected to stay in Health Conservation 21 until we were twenty-one years old, at which point we were supposed to enter a sheltered workshop.

The kids in my class ranged in age from nine to twenty-one. All of us were forced to rest after lunch, including Joanie LaPadula, the girl with the brown ponytail, and Jill Kirschner, the other older girl. Given that we got pulled from class for physical therapy, occupational therapy and/or speech therapy, our instructional time added up to less than three hours a day. Which is partly why, at eighteen and nineteen, respectively, Joanie and Jill didn't know how to read very well.

Not only were we not required to participate in the American system of education; we were actually blocked from it and hidden away in the basement.

But from my nine-year-old perspective, Health Conservation 21 was a whole new world, and I was so happy to no longer be sitting at home every day.

I STARTED SCHOOL right at a time when things were starting to change. Parents' expectations for their children with disabilities were challenging the status quo. Some of the students in the program had parents who were more like mine, parents who expected that their children would complete school, go to college, and get a job. My mother and father rightly worried that Health Conservation 21 was teaching me almost nothing, especially since I was already reading at a high school level and clearly needed an academic challenge. But they decided that it was better for me to attend Health Conservation 21 than not go to school at all.

Even though we were glad to be in school, at the same time my peers and I were becoming conscious of feeling dismissed, categorized as unteachable, and extraneous to society. For the first time we were able to describe feelings we'd secretly had for a long time but had been unable to put into words. I confided how uncomfortable I felt when people stared at me, and my frustration about having to wear what my mother had picked out instead of what I wanted because I couldn't get to my closet. It was a huge discovery when I found that my new friends felt the same way I did. We spent hours trying to figure out why we were treated so differently from the kids upstairs. We talked about our rest period and wondered why we had to have it, since it just took time away from learning.

Unintentionally, the time we spent together at Health Conservation 21—our bonding in the face of exclusion—was teaching us something that would become essential to our success later. We were learning that despite what society might be telling us, we all had something to contribute: Steve was always a jokester; Neil was great in math; Nancy was a loving friend with a beautiful smile and a strong spirit. We shared similar goals, had similar struggles, and as we continued to grow in the future, we would come to support each other in our dreams of what we wanted our lives to become.

Now I know that what we were all beginning to learn was what today might be called disability culture. Although "disability culture" is really just a term for a culture that has learned to value the humanity in all people, without dismissing anyone for looking, thinking, believing, or acting differently. Like Buddhism. Or kid culture. Because we were kids doing what kids naturally do until they are taught otherwise: Slow down enough to listen and truly see each other. Ask questions. Connect. Find a way to have fun. Learn.

On Fridays after school I started hanging out with two new friends, Frieda and Linda. Linda was Jewish and had muscular dystrophy. We'd get together and talk for hours and hours and hours. But it was with Frieda that I bonded most strongly. Frieda was a year or two younger than me, but it never mattered. She was very smart and articulate and we talked about everything. Her parents were also Jewish, and also survivors. They'd lived through the war in Poland by hiding in sewers. They also lived in

Brooklyn, where her father was in a union and they were social-
ists. At home the whole family spoke Yiddish. When Frieda and I
inched along the sidewalk in our wheelchairs outside one of our
houses, people stared at us, as usual. Instead of ignoring them,
though, as we normally did, we turned around and talked back
to them.

"Take a picture. It will last longer!" we'd say and fall apart
giggling.

Looking back now, I don't know what would have happened
if I hadn't started school at that time—in the aftermath of the
candy store incident and the feeling that I no longer belonged
in the circle of my block. Frieda and I were segregated and excluded, and only our parents expected anything of us, but we had
found each other.

The summer after I started Health Conservation 21, I went to
a summer camp for kids with disabilities. My mother had heard
about Camp Oakhurst from one of the other mothers, and my
parents had decided to send me. This was the beginning of my
ten-year love affair with camp.

In one of my earliest camp memories, I am Peter Pan in the
camp play. In my Peter Pan costume I am wearing a green hat and
have green booties on my feet. Sarah is Wendy. Sarah has cerebral
palsy, and her struggle to articulate her words stretches her lines
out into long, heartfelt sentences. But no one cares how long
it takes because Sarah has transformed into the perfect Wendy,
and June is an impish pixie Tinkerbell in leg braces and crutches.
In my role as Peter Pan, I sing so loudly and beautifully that the
entire camp is quiet, listening to me. My song is about childhood
and my love of independence and freedom. I feel Peter Pan's love
of independence deep in my soul because I, too, have this feeling,
perhaps for the first time and this is a new feeling.

At camp we tasted freedom for the first time in our lives.
Camp is where we had freedom from our parents dressing us,

choosing our clothes for us, choosing our food for us, driving us to our friends' houses. This is something we would have naturally grown out of, like our nondisabled friends, but we live in an inaccessible world, so we have not. We loved our parents but we relished our freedom from them.

I met my first boyfriend at camp. His name was Esteban and he was from Puerto Rico. He had muscular dystrophy and rode in a wheelchair just like mine, which he was unable to push by himself. We both had to be pushed by others. He had a shock of brown curly hair and we liked to talk together. On movie night he took my hand from my lap and held it and we sat, holding hands, watching the films.

The freedom we felt at camp was not just from our parents and our need for their daily assistance in order to live our lives.

We were drunk on the freedom of not feeling like a burden, a feeling that was a constant companion in our lives outside of camp.

Take the summer my mother signed me up for Bible school. This might sound strange for a Jewish child, but she did it because it was an educational activity that would connect me with other kids, the kind of thing she was constantly on the lookout for before I started school. At this Bible school, we sang and played games and did all the things you might expect at a summer Bible school program, which I liked and enjoyed. But there was a part of the day, a very small part, when some kind of activity happened in the basement, which of course I couldn't get to, which meant I couldn't participate in it. My parents and I were used to accepting these types of barriers, so my mother didn't say anything about it. We would have accepted that for this small portion of the day I would not be a part of things. But the pastor, who was very kind, offered to carry me down the stairs. A fairly easy thing for him to do, given how small and light I was at the time. My mother, however, stopped him. She told him it wasn't necessary, that I'd be okay not being with the other kids in the basement.

Now why would my mother, a woman who spent half her life working to overcome barriers for me, have declined an offer to have me included in an activity?

Because she worried I would be a burden.

My mother worried that if having me in the program became too difficult, the pastor might decide the effort wasn't worth it and wouldn't want me back. My mother straddled a fine line between fighting to not have me excluded and worrying that she'd pushed so hard for inclusion that I'd end up excluded. At Bible school we were lucky. The pastor was the kind of guy who understood that if all the kids were doing something it would be weird for me not to do it, too, so he carried me up and down the stairs, despite my mother telling him it wasn't necessary. Which I know made my mother happy.

But the bottom line is this: My mother worried when my needs became a burden. So I thought of myself and my needs as a burden too. I just kind of accepted it.

Even though my mother definitely pushed on things, there were certain areas she *didn't* push. Like, because it was inconvenient for the pastor to carry me down the stairs and he didn't really have to do it, and they weren't going to be down there a long time anyway, it would be all right if I didn't go—so let's not push this issue. In this case, the pastor was a nice guy so he did it anyway, but above all, you did not want your kid to become a burden. Which meant the parents needed us kids to adjust and accept not participating—and we learned to do this. We accepted that our inclusion was dependent on someone else being "nice."

Getting into Health Conservation 21 felt the same way. It was not like regular school, where you were required to go to school and automatically accepted; you had to be screened. You were given all these assessments and then people actually voted on whether or not they would accept you into the program. Although I don't think anybody was ever not accepted, there was always the sense that they didn't have to take you and if they wanted to get rid of you, they could.

But camp was completely different. Camp was for us. It was designed specifically with our needs in mind and our parents paid for us to be a part of it. Our participation wasn't contingent on someone else's generosity; it was a given. I didn't have to worry that if I wanted to do something or go someplace, I'd have to ask somebody for a favor. I didn't have to feel guilty about how much work it took to get me dressed and take me to the bathroom. The counselors were paid to do these things for us, which made all the difference in the world. Because the reality is, asking people to do something for you when you're not paying them or they're not required to do it in some way means that you are asking someone for a favor. And doing favors for someone gets old. Favors mean that someone has to stop what they're doing, whatever it is, in order to help you with what you're doing, which always feels like an interruption, an intrusion.

At camp I didn't have to worry about what I needed, or how much help I could ask for at one time. I didn't have to secretly rank what I needed in order of importance so as not to ask for too much at once. I didn't have to feel that bad feeling I got when something was inaccessible and someone said no to something I knew I could have done myself if my whole world had been accessible.

Camp, I thought, was what it would feel like if society included us.

CHAPTER 2

INSUBORDINATE

THE PENCIL WAS SLIPPERY in the grip of my clammy hands, and my heart pounded with anxiety. "Everyone has to get used to taking exams sometime," I told myself.

"Just not at fourteen," a voice deep inside me answered.

It was 1961 and I was at Sheepshead Bay High School. My mother and a group of the other disabled kids' mothers had successfully pushed the school district into making a number of schools in each borough wheelchair accessible with support staff. I was the first student from P.S. 219's Health Conservation 21 to go to high school.

This meant I was facing real expectations, real grades, and real exams for the first time in my life.

I took a breath and tried to calm down. It wasn't that I hadn't studied; I'd studied for weeks. The minute hand on the classroom clock ticked loudly in the silence of twenty-five students concentrating. I looked up at it. Thirty minutes left.

I had to pee. I shouldn't have had that glass of water with my sandwich at lunch. I was used to rationing my water intake when I knew there wouldn't be anyone to help me go to the bathroom, but because I'd skipped drinking at breakfast I'd thought it would be okay. I was wrong. Ugh.

Forcing myself to stop thinking about my aching "I have to pee" sensation, I put my head back down and kept writing.

The bell rang just as I was finishing my last sentence. The room erupted into movement—slamming books, zipping bags, dragging chairs. All around me, I could hear bursts of exclamations.

"Hey, Scott, how about that exam, huh?"

"Kim, wait for me!"

"John, you going to football after school?"

In the midst of it, I sat quietly toying with my pencil, my test anxiety giving away to the habitual self-consciousness I felt each time the bell rang and I had to face the halls at school. I was getting bused an hour and a half across Brooklyn to Sheepshead Bay because my neighborhood high school wasn't accessible. Sheepshead Bay was basically a fishing village on the edge of New York City. The kids grew up in a tight-knit group, swimming in the harbor and playing baseball. And I didn't know any of them.

And now I had to ask one of them to help me get to my next class.

Waiting for the tumult to subside so I wouldn't have to shout for a favor over the noise, I sat quietly. Not wanting to look as lonely as I felt, I pretended to look for something in my bag. Finally, the uproar calmed. I glanced around the room to see who was left. Across from me, gathering her books, was a girl from my seventh-period math class. I'd noticed her because she always asked good questions. What was her name again? I tried desperately to remember. Sarah? Stella? Sally?

"Um, excuse me. Sorry. I wonder if . . . Would you mind . . . Could I ask, if you might help me get to my next class?" In my nervousness, I stumbled over my words.

"Sure!" The girl looked up at me and quickly smiled brightly. A little too brightly. "I'm going to English. Room 312. Where are you going?"

"Oh darn it! I'm going to room 207. History. A whole floor below. Out of your way, I'm sure. I'm sorry. I hope I don't make you late, but, uh, do you mind if we stop at the bathroom on the way?" A blush rose on my face. It was so uncomfortable.

"Of course!" the girl chirped, as she walked behind my wheel-chair to wheel me out the door.

Entering the hallway, I looked straight ahead and asked the girl her name. It was Sally. This was one of my tricks. If I focused on the girl and didn't look around me, I wouldn't see all the chatting and socializing that left me feeling excluded.

By the time I got to Sheepshead Bay, I'd spent all the years of my school life at Health Conservation 21 and my summers at camp—cloistered in a world of kids with disabilities. My sudden immersion in the tidal wave of nondisabled kids unnerved me: they moved so quickly through the halls, carrying books, talking and shouting to each other, bantering, making after-school plans. And none of it could I do. Between having to get pushed to my classrooms and bused an hour and a half to and from school, there was little room left for socializing in the little pockets of time kids normally find during the day. Neither did I have much confidence in my ability to break into a conversation. Or even start one. First of all, my chair put my face at exactly butt height, which made talking hard if someone didn't think to bend down. Second, for the first time in my life, I was in a competitive school and my anxiety about measuring up made it hard for me to relax. Then, on top of everything else, the nondisabled kids had a way of interacting in class and telling jokes that felt unfamiliar. It was as if I'd lived my life speaking a different language, in a completely different culture. The separation of my "disabled world" and my "regular world" had created a chasm that I now had to bridge, which made me feel as if I had to become two Judys. My cloistered years at Health Conservation 21 had made me supremely confident about my place in my disabled world, but I was insecure in the regular world. I knew about the nondisabled world from my block, but the kids at my new high school—unlike the kids I'd known forever from my street, and the kids I knew from adult-facilitated activities, like Hebrew School and Brownies—didn't seem to be used to interacting with a kid in a wheelchair. As far as I could tell, they didn't see me as a normal teenage girl who it might be fun to hang out with. And as I grew increasingly interested in boys, I realized that they didn't seem to see me as a possible girlfriend.

No one expected me to date. I was "crippled" and was often told, whether explicitly and implicitly, that no boy would ever give me a second look. It was as if I was seen as a kind of non-sex. When kids looked at me, I felt like all they saw was my wheelchair. Nothing else. They weren't even ignoring me; I could tell by the way they looked right through me. They just didn't even register my presence. It was as if they unconsciously categorized me as a nonentity.

From my time at camp, though, I knew what it felt like to be treated like a regular girl.

At camp, I was not seen as a sick kid, excluded from dances and dates and kissing boys behind the football stadium. Nor was I seen as a crippled girl never expected to marry, for whom motherhood was not even a question. No one had told me that no boy would ever give me a second look. At camp we had parties, played loud rock music, and snuck off into the dark to make out. The counselors were young and fun. They strummed the guitar while we sang and danced to the likes of Elvis Presley, Chubby Checker, Buddy Holly, Sam Cooke, and the Shirelles. We knew all the words to "Itsy Bitsy Teenie Weenie Yellow Polka Dot Bikini" and "Chantilly Lace" by the Big Bopper, and we danced in a way we never danced anywhere else. Camp was the only place we weren't self-conscious about how we looked.

But we Heumanns are taught not to accept barriers. We keep moving forward. So, during my hour-and-a-half bus ride to and

from school and in my smaller special-ed classes, I made friends
with the other disabled kids. There may have only been nine or
ten of us in my entire grade, but when we came together it gave
me the strength to face the rest of my classes with the regular
kids. At home, my neighborhood friends had stopped playing on
the block; they'd moved on to doing things I couldn't do, like
hanging out at soda shops and going to the movies. Increasingly,
I relied on the telephone to connect with people. It was the telephone that saved me from feeling lonely.

The funny, not funny, thing about being told that I should
never expect to get married is that ultimately it resulted in my
being pushed to achieve in school.

At a time when many women were encouraged to think about
going to college only as a potential route to getting their "Mrs."
degree, that is, finding a spouse, the message I got was the opposite. I would *not* be able to count on getting married and having a husband who would take care of me. "You need to be able
to support yourself, and you aren't going to be able to support
yourself on a high school degree, so you have to go to college,"
my mother would tell me. Which was a gift, because my parents
hadn't gone to college and we lived in a neighborhood where
many of our neighbors hadn't either—and, of course, I was a
woman at a time when women weren't expected to continue
their education after high school. Neither Mary nor Arlene, nor
most of my female cousins, were planning on going to college. To
be fair, it wasn't just the messages around my marriage prospects
that pushed me—education had always been very important to
my parents. The way they saw it, their job was to work and take
care of us, and our job was to go to school and get good grades.

So in high school, I didn't date. I talked on the phone and I
studied. I studied so hard, in fact, that by the time I graduated I
found that I'd won an award.

Because there were too many students to have our graduation ceremony at the school in Sheepshead Bay, it was held at Brooklyn College.

I sat in the back of our car, my father driving our family to Brooklyn College to watch me get up onstage to receive my award, and I couldn't stop beaming. I was proud. Despite all the lonely moments, the embarrassment, the hard work, the test anxiety, and the fear of failure, I'd hung in there. Glancing back at me, my mother smiled. I knew she and my dad were proud too. After all the nos, all the people who'd said, "No, Judy's not welcome here," and all the fighting, I was finally graduating from high school and had been accepted at Long Island University.

Pulling into a parking spot as close to the college as he could find, my dad stopped the car. Joey pushed the side door open and my brothers climbed out into the street, while I sat and waited for my dad to roll my chair down the ramp to the ground. I felt good in my floral dress and black graduate robes, my long hair falling past my shoulders. I could see that my aunt and uncle had found my mother and they clustered in a little group on the sidewalk, chatting.

Inside Brooklyn College, the giant hall was bursting. There were families taking pictures of graduates in their hats and robes, arms draped around each other, grinning, grandparents standing together, while little brothers and sisters chased each other through the crowd. Cautiously, my father pushed me through the crowd toward the stage. The kids getting awards were supposed to sit on the stage so they could easily be called forward and congratulated in front of the audience.

"Sorry . . . Excuse me . . . Sorry . . . Excuse me," my father and I slowly wound our way through the hall. My mother, brothers, aunt, uncle and cousins peeled off to find seats. From my chair I couldn't see much, but my father targeted the left side of the room. As we drew closer, the crowd thinned out and I spotted the stairs on the stage. Right away, I saw the problem: there was no ramp.

"Dad, there's no ramp," I said, trying not to get anxious.

"Hmmmm. Maybe there's one around the back," my father said noncommittally, refusing to get worked up. Pushing me to the bottom of the stairs, he turned to a security guard.

"Excuse me, sir, is there a ramp to access the stage? My daughter is receiving an award and she's supposed to sit on the stage." Waiting for the man to answer, my heart pounded. Please please please let there be a ramp. I did not want to get carried onto the stage in front of this huge crowd. Nor did I want to watch my father bump and lug my wheelchair up the stairs after me.

Looking at me, the guard shook his head. "No, sir, sorry. No ramp. Just stairs."

My heart sank. My father sighed a very quiet sigh.

Decisively, he pulled my wheelchair to the side of the stairs.

"Okay, honey. I'll pull your wheelchair up like I always do." He turned my chair around and started to mount the stairs. Fighting a sense of embarrassment, not wanting to see how many people might be witnessing my awkward entry onto the stage, I took a breath and looked straight ahead.

Which is why I didn't notice the principal until he called out to my father. "Sir! Mr. Heumann! Wait a minute. Just leave Judy down here in the front row. She doesn't need to be onstage."

"What?" My father paused halfway up the stairs, disbelieving. "It's no problem. I'm happy to bring her up."

"No, no, it's not necessary." The principal shook his head.

My father looked confused and unhappy. I felt my face grow hot. I wanted to disappear.

"Look," my father said to the principal, "it's very easy. I'll just put her wheelchair on the stage. It will take two minutes."

The principal looked at my father. "No," he said firmly. "Judy does not need to be on the stage. Put her in the front row." It was obvious. The principal did not want me on the stage. I felt nauseated.

"Dad, let's go home," I said. "I don't want to stay." Tears came to my eyes.

My father squared his shoulders and seemed to grow in height. He became the ex-marine who'd fought at Iwo Jima and won a Purple Heart.

"I am going to take Judy up the stairs and put her on the stage," he told the principal, enunciating every word slowly with a deathly calm. "So she can receive her award on the stage. With all the other kids." I froze and looked at the principal. What would he say?

For a long moment the principal didn't speak. Finally, he conceded. "Take her up," he said.

I couldn't stop my tears. I was utterly humiliated. "Dad," I said, "I want to go home. Take me home."

"No, Judy." My father was stern. "You are not going home. You are going to stay here. You are going to sit on the stage and receive your award. You worked hard. It is your award and you deserve it." He climbed the rest of the steps to the stage and pushed me to a spot on the stage.

I took a deep breath, trying to compose myself. He was right. This was my award, and even though not one part of me felt like it, I knew I belonged here. I straightened my hair band and wiped my eyes.

As my father stood next to me, the principal walked over to us.

"Put her here," he said, motioning to an empty spot behind the rest of the students on the stage. He might be acquiescing to my father, but he wanted me in the back. He did not want me to be seen.

My father was not happy. He clenched his jaw and his mouth tightened. But he wheeled me to the back of the stage where the principal had indicated. I fought back new tears.

"Good luck, honey. We'll be watching." Kissing the top of my head, he left. I looked out at the masses in the audience. I would not cry in front of all these people.

"I belong here," I repeated to myself silently.

When the principal called my name and started to walk to the back of the stage, I was slowly pushing my wheelchair toward the front of the stage but only made it a little ways forward before he intercepted me and handed me my award.

I looked him directly in the eyes.

"Thank you," I said.

But of course no one heard me.

The following September I started at Long Island University, which was about a twenty-minute drive from my parents' home in Brooklyn.

At LIU, I decided to major in speech therapy, but not because I wanted to be a speech therapist. I wanted to be a teacher. The problem was, I didn't think it would be a good idea to major in education because I was afraid that if I did, I'd lose the funding that supported my education. Through a program originally developed to support returning disabled World War I veterans in finding work, the US Office of Vocational Rehabilitation paid for my college expenses. The Office of Vocational Rehabilitation, or "Rehab," as we called it, helped disabled people prepare for and obtain employment. Friends had warned me about Rehab's take on what they considered realistic careers to be for disabled people.

"Don't tell Rehab you want to be a teacher," my friends told me, "because if you tell them that you want to be a teacher, they'll tell you you can't because nobody else is a teacher who's in a wheelchair." In other words, if you couldn't show Rehab that there was someone who had a disability similar to yours working in a profession like the one you wanted to study for, then they wouldn't pay for it. So I had to choose a major that would be considered "acceptable" to Rehab which is where the speech therapy came in—and figure out a different route to becoming a teacher.

As luck would have it, it was the 1960s, and the postwar baby boom had created such a demand for teachers that the Board of Education was accepting people with fewer credits in education. I could minor in education and still be considered eligible to teach. I majored in speech and theater, because I loved musical theater, and took classes in education, speech, and musical theater. When I met with Rehab, I told them that I wanted to be a speech therapist, mentioning nothing about my interest in education. In response, they gave me a battery of tests that said I had the personality of a social worker, which they tried to push me into doing. But my parents intervened. "Look, she wants to be a speech therapist. Let her be a speech therapist." And because there were other speech therapists with disabilities, Rehab relented.

Unfortunately, Rehab wasn't the only obstacle on my radar. The New York City Board of Education had never before hired a teacher who used a wheelchair, and, as I knew from my childhood, they had a pretty dim view of people who used wheelchairs. I suspected they would be unlikely to grant me a teaching license when the time came. Preemptively I called the American Civil Liberties Union.

"I'm interested in being a teacher," I told the ACLU, "but I've never met or heard of any teachers who are wheelchair users. Is there anything you suggest I do?"

"Well, just go ahead and take the courses that you need," they responded. "And if you have a problem, call us." That was my freshman year.

I LIVED IN A COLLEGE DORM. LIU was a small campus, only three
or four main buildings, and most of the students commuted to
school, but I thought I would get more out of my college experience if I lived on campus. It also would have been very difficult
for me to commute back and forth from home because neither
the bus nor the train system in New York was wheelchair accessible. I had already spent years commuting to elementary, middle,
and high school, which was partly what contributed to my feeling so alienated from my fellow students in high school—I did
not want that again in college.

The dorm I lived in had two steps into the building, no ramp,
and a step into the bathroom—and I did not yet have a motorized wheelchair. This meant that every day, every time I had to
go to the bathroom, or into my dorm, or to class, I had to ask
somebody to help me up the steps, or push me to where I was
going. Usually, I tried to get someone I knew to push me, but
sometimes I would just ask a stranger. Fortunately, the campus
was small, so the lack of access was confined to a small area,
which is one of the reasons I had chosen LIU. Of course, I was
used to asking for this kind of help.

The bigger challenge to living alone in the dorms, however,
was in the morning and at night, when I needed help getting my
braces on and off, getting dressed or undressed, and in and out of
bed. During the summer before my freshman year, a friend from
camp who was a year ahead of me at LIU had connected me with
a female student who she thought might be willing to help me
out. Which is how I met my lifelong friend Toni, whom I roomed
with my first year. Toni, who was from New Mexico, went to
Barnard College in uptown Manhattan, but due to a shortage
of accommodation at Barnard she had been placed in a dorm
at LIU.

But Toni wasn't around during the day, only in mornings and
evenings—and if she had something to do in the evenings, which

she often did, she got home late at night. All of which meant I had to be resourceful about how I went to the bathroom and got to class.

I made friends on the floor I lived on, and there were some people who would help me when I needed it. I developed a certain kind of radar about whom I could ask for help. I could tell right away that certain people would be very unlikely to say no, not because they felt guilty, but because they were just, like, "Sure, of course I'll help you," whereas there were certain other people I just wouldn't ask at all. And then there were some people whom I would ask only if absolutely necessary, because I had no idea which way it might go—it felt like I could ask and they might say yes, but they might just as easily say no. I really didn't like asking those people because if I had to ask them something like "Could you help me go to the bathroom?" you just got the sense that it was going to be uncomfortable.

Even though I was used to asking for help, I didn't *like* asking for help. I always felt as though asking for help meant that I wasn't doing something well enough for myself, even though I was physically unable to push myself to class or up a step. I worried about what would happen if I had to go to the bathroom and no one was around to help me. What would I do? I did anything I could to avoid having to go to the bathroom and tried to drink as few liquids as possible. I did a lot of planning, thinking about what I would drink, who would be around to assist me if I had to go to the bathroom, and whether they had a test or something else that made them unavailable. In fact, I still do a certain level of this today to be sure I don't get caught out with no way to go to the bathroom, but back then I was completely dependent on my ability to strategize and ask for favors.

In retrospect I see that this was inhibiting to my natural extroversion—I probably would have been much more outgoing at that time if I hadn't been so reliant on favors. As it was, I had to push myself into situations where I would be forced to interact with new people. I never would have gone out for a sorority except that a friend from camp was in one at Syracuse University and she recommended me to the LIU chapter of her sorority. The sorority building had steps, so I had to be carried in and out of the building, but being a pledge meant that I *had* to go out a certain number of hours a day, I had to be at our information table a certain number of hours a day, and there were certain things I was required to participate in and do.

Still, I was often lonely. I had my friends Eileen and Lois, who lived on my floor, and a couple of others, and that was good, but I was never fully included in things. At a time and place when people tend to date like mad, I didn't date. I had romantic relationships at camp and in my disabled community, but not in college. In fact, I didn't go on one single date with anyone I knew from college the entire time I was in college.

One time I had an experience when I was alone in my room on a weekend night and someone knocked on my door. I used to go home on weekends, but this particular weekend I didn't, for some reason.

At the door was another student, a boy I recognized but didn't know.

"Hi!" he said brightly. "Sorry to bother you, but I was just wondering, um, we're going on a triple date and one of the women who was supposed to come can't come. Do you know anyone who is around tonight and could take her place?"

Speechless, I sat in the doorway. The wind was completely knocked out of me. For a moment, every particle of my being wished I'd heard something entirely different, wished that he'd actually been inviting me on a triple date. That I could say, "Yes! I am free. I would love to go!"

But the way he looked at me, with such innocent inquiry and expectation, just hoping that I might know some other woman, *any* other woman, who might like to join a group at the last minute, made me feel like all I could say was, "No, not really," and then quietly close the door and turn around in my empty room. I was confused and heart-wrenchingly sad to the point of numbness. I just couldn't understand what I had to do to be seen as an ordinary person.

Deep inside, a part of me was slowly giving up on the hope of ever feeling fully accepted by the nondisabled world.

I drew closer to the students with disabilities. One of the things I liked about LIU was that there was a community of disabled students. We talked a lot about wanting the university to become more accessible. The steps in and out of the dorm and in and out of the bathrooms were not very convenient, to say the least. But not everyone agreed about how to handle the issue of accessibility. The head of the school of psychology was quoted in a school newspaper article as saying that it would be better if disabled students didn't go to LIU at all because it was psychologically traumatic for us to be in an inaccessible environment.

I recognize now that exclusion, especially at the level and frequency at which I experienced it, *is* traumatic. Although at the time it didn't feel out of the bounds of my normal, everyday experience—I can see that constantly coping with it definitely impacted me and it never stopped being painful. Interestingly, though, my reaction to being left out was not to become angry or aggressive toward people, which is a common reaction to feeling excluded, especially when you feel you lack control over your life. Perhaps this was due to the fact that because I didn't accept my lack of control, I didn't accept the idea that we couldn't change things. Nor did I internalize the exclusion and attribute it to an internal deficiency on my part. I just didn't at all accept feeling permanently left out of the world.

It was around that time that my friends and I were starting to differ from our parents in our take on the barriers we faced. Our parents' generation associated disability with President Franklin Roosevelt, who actively hid from the public his paralysis from polio. He never allowed himself to be photographed in his wheelchair or being helped with his mobility. He talked about disability as something for an individual to beat or conquer. We disagreed with this—we did not see our issue as a medical problem that, if we just "fixed" it, would be fine. We were beginning to see our lack of access as a problem with society, rather than our individual problem. From our perspective, disability was something that could happen to anyone at any time, and frequently did, so it was right for society to design its infrastructure and systems around this fact of life. We had grown up with the civil rights movement. I was eight when Rosa Parks refused to give up her seat in the whites-only section of the bus and just starting college when the Civil Rights Act was passed in 1964. Wasn't it the government's responsibility to ensure that everyone could participate equally in our society?

I ENDED UP getting more and more drawn to politics. It pulled me out of my shell and, as I started to meet more people, I became more of my normal sociable self.

I ran for student council and won.

"No," I said, speaking into the telephone, which was sitting next to where I was lying in my parents' dining room in a hospital bed, "if we're going to fight the tuition hike, we have to build more support before we meet with the dean."

"I agree," said the student council president. "Why don't we call a meeting of the full council to strategize?"

Saying goodbye to the president, I clicked the speaker button and hung up the phone.

"Mom," I called, "can you turn me when you have a minute?" I had to take a few notes on my conversation with the president and could do that much more easily if I was turned so that I faced the bed rather than lying with my back to the bed.

It was winter of my junior year, and I was encased in a body cast from my shoulders to my knees. My long hair had been cut short and I had had four holes drilled into my head, where the doctors had attached a metal crown with four screws. On my cast were two big metal hoops, which my parents and friends used to turn me. I'd had two surgeries to fuse my spine just after New Year's, which was supposed to prevent further curvature of my spine. But the recovery was long. I was supposed to remain in the dining room until June, and it was only February.

I'd run for junior-class secretary the year before and had lost, but just after my surgery my competitor had quit. With the help of my friends, I ran again from my spot in my parents' dining room, and won. Needless to say, I was on the telephone all the time. And even though I was immobilized at home, the student council president and I worked well together.

The student government at LIU was very different from what it had been when I started college. When I'd started my freshman year, it had been run by the sororities and fraternities. But the Vietnam War was fast changing things. Over the past two years the war had expanded to the point where, as of November of my junior year, forty thousand men were getting drafted every month. People were dying, and many, many more were coming home wounded. The antiwar movement was spreading, and student activism at LIU had grown, as it had on many other college campuses. This in turn had sparked interest in student government, and the LIU student council had been taken over by students active in the antiwar movement, of which I was one.

"Thanks, Mom," I said, as my mother came out of the kitchen and rotated me.

My mother's activism was increasing, too. She had always been a tremendous advocate for my education and a regular volunteer at our synagogue, organizing lunches and events. Now she had also become involved in the neighborhood. When a black

family moved in, an occurrence to which some of our white
neighbors reacted unhappily, grumbling about the neighborhood
going downhill, my mother spoke up for the family. She encouraged people to try and see things differently. Although the majority in our neighborhood was still white, and it would be years
before the neighborhood would really shift demographically, she
was already an early advocate against the flight of white people to
the suburbs. Of course, she did this in her own quiet way.

Meanwhile, I was preoccupied with my antiwar work and
my position on the student council. Despite my immobility
on the table, I was taking nearly a full load of classes. I used a
telephone-like machine called Executone that my friends moved
from class to class for me, so that I could listen in on lectures.
When I wanted to ask a question I just clicked a button to let the
professor know that I wanted to participate. Ironically, sometimes I felt more integrated into the regular world from my spot
in the dining room than I did at school. Yes, I missed being on
campus, but there was something freeing about being able to
connect with people and participate in class without having to
constantly worry about asking for the favor of a push or help to
the bathroom. Plus, being junior-class secretary gave me a clear
role in the "regular" world. It made me integral to meetings and
events, which made me feel accepted and included. All of this
combined to give me an unexpected sense of belonging.

DURING MY SENIOR YEAR at LIU, I spent much of my time at an
after-school tutoring clinic I started with a new friend, Tony, a
fellow aspiring teacher. Trying to get teaching experience with
children, in preparation for graduation, Tony and I ran a program to help kids with their homework. Working with the kids
from Fort Greene, I found I had an aptitude for connecting with
children. I enjoyed speaking with them and learning about their
lives, as I sat with them and explained concepts or corrected

math problems. As the year passed, however, I felt myself getting more and more worried about what was going to happen when I graduated and it came time to get my teaching license. To do so I would have to undergo a medical exam to ensure I was healthy and didn't have any communicable diseases, in addition to the other exams I had had to take.

Just five steps led up to the brass-plated double front doors of the New York City Board of Education building at 110 Livingston Street, but I didn't bother to count the steps just then. It could have been twenty-five or ten or two and it wouldn't have mattered. All I knew was that there were steps, and I'd prepared accordingly. Luckily, Tony had been a willing recruit for my mission. Pausing at the bottom of the stairs, he looked at me now.

"Ready?" he asked.

I nodded. I was ready.

"Here we go!" Tony smiled at me and then turned me around, grasped the black handles of my wheelchair, and pulled me up the stairs and into the building backward.

I had recently gotten a Motorette for my manual wheelchair, which made it electric. We reengaged the motor now and I wheeled into the lobby. The lobby was vast and ornate, not quite what one would expect for a government building, but I didn't have time to look. I rolled my chair to the reception desk and looked up at the man in uniform behind the counter.

"I'm here to see Dr. James."

"Third floor, number 312. Sign here, please." The man sounded bored.

The buttons in the wood-paneled elevator were out of my reach, as usual, which was another one of the reasons Tony was there. He pressed the button, and we waited for the elevator to arrive. It was slow and creaky, and I could hear it lumbering its way down the shaft from the upper reaches of the building. Closing my eyes, I took a deep breath. I was sure Tony could feel my nervousness. I had no confidence that this medical exam would be routine in any way. I'd passed the oral and written exams—this doctor's appointment was the last test standing between me and my teaching credentials. It was supposed to be a routine exam to determine whether I had any medical issues that made me a danger to children. Should be simple. It was standard for all prospective teachers, and I was in good health. I knew that what I was asking to do was perfectly reasonable; all I wanted to do was teach.

But anxiety gripped my stomach. I just couldn't bring myself to believe that I'd be treated fairly. Nothing about school had ever been simple or routine for me.

I tightened my grasp on my armrest and tried to think of every possible question the doctor could ask me.

The elevator door slid open. I wheeled inside, and Tony pressed the button for the third floor.

The elevator slogged its way up, past the second floor and stopped. The door slowly slid open. Quietly, Tony and I glanced down the hall, looking for room 312. Tony pushed the heavy door open so I could maneuver my chair into the office.

"I'm here to see Dr. James," I informed the woman behind the reception desk.

The woman shuffled through some papers and looked up. "Judy Heumann?"

"Yes," I responded.

"Please wait here."

I rolled to the side of the desk and tried to settle myself, too nervous to page through magazines or say anything to Tony. The door next to the reception desk opened and an older woman poked her head into the room.

"Judy Heumann?" she called with a questioning tone as she looked around. She was of average height and weight, with short gray hair pressed against her head in a fashion from the previous decade. She had a tight, reserved smile, her sensible shoes silent on the floor.

"Yes, that's me," I said. I drove myself in her direction. The woman offered her hand, her eyes taking me in, from my long straight brown hair and bangs to my platform shoes resting on my wheelchair.

"I'm Dr. James," she said and ushered me into a small office, where she took a seat at a brown wooden desk in the corner.

At first the medical exam was more or less predictable. Dr. James took my blood pressure, listened to my heart, and asked standard questions. All normal. I relaxed a little. The doctor moved on, asking questions about the history of my polio. I'd been eighteen months old when I contracted the virus and was sick for about a month. I was in an iron lung for three months, and the illness had left me quadriplegic: unable to walk, with only limited use of my hands and arms.

Gradually the doctor's questioning became more pointed and intense. An almost voyeuristic titillation seemed to enter her demeanor, as she asked about my polio-related medical treatment from twenty years ago. As I complied, describing in detail the two surgeries I'd had and the rehabilitation I'd done after polio, I started to grow increasingly uncomfortable. Things were starting to feel wrong. Some boundary was being crossed.

Yes, I'd been in and out of the hospital until I was five. At six, I'd had a surgery to release the tendons in my knees and hips, and just recently I'd had a spinal fusion. I was sure this line of inquiry was completely irrelevant to whether or not I was a medical danger to second graders while sitting in a classroom teaching them English.

"Yes, yes, mmmm. Raise your arms," the doctor continued. I lifted my forearms up as far as I could, with my elbows on the armrests of my chair. I can't lift my arms, and told the doctor this, though I still didn't understand the relevance of the instruction.

Had I ever walked, the doctor wanted to know. My anxiety piqued. Familiar alarm bells started clanging in my head. This was definitely out of the bounds of what was appropriate and pertinent.

"Well, before my spinal fusion I used braces and crutches to stand, but I've never really walked." I had never walked across a street.

Then, in a matter-of-fact voice, in the same exact tone that she'd asked me to breathe in and breathe out, the doctor asked me to show her how I went to the bathroom.

The unexpected question socked me in the stomach.

This was wrong, completely inappropriate. Hot angry tears came to my eyes. This should not be happening.

But of course it was.

What could I possibly say? I fought the urge to wheel around and drive out.

I had no choice but to answer.

Years of managing my feelings in the face of bold stares and invasive personal questions had honed my ability to keep a calm front. I managed to hold on to some amount of composure.

"Well," I told the doctor, my voice cracking, "if other teachers are going to have to show their students how to go to the bathroom, then of course I'll do it, but otherwise you can be assured that I can take care of it myself." I was slightly stunned at my adept answer. I'd had no idea that that retort was going to come out of my mouth.

The doctor shifted her eyes away from me and didn't respond, but moved on and returned to the subject of my walking.

"Tell me again how you walk," she said.

I tried to explain again that I'd never walked independently. I'd been in a wheelchair since I was two and had never been able to stand up or sit down by myself. I reiterated that since I could not really walk, putting me in a classroom with braces and crutches would not be safe for me or my students. My motorized wheelchair solved any mobility challenge.

My explanation didn't seem to reach her. Dr. James wrote a short note in her folder, snapped it closed, and told me to come back for a second appointment, this time wearing my braces and bringing my crutches to show her how I walked.

The appointment was over.

I was past tears. Fury churned in my chest. I'd worried that something bad might happen, called the ACLU, tried to plan for every possible outcome, but had never thought of anything like this. This was beyond what I ever could have even imagined. I was shocked and disgusted.

I felt totally alone. She could do anything she wanted to me, say anything she wanted to me, and there was nothing I could do about it. There were no rules. No boundaries.

This was what discrimination felt like.

In the doctor's waiting room, trying through my tears and anger to keep my voice low and even, I told Tony we were leaving,

In the elevator I explained what had happened. He was outraged for me, but what was there to say? He knew that this kind of treatment was not unusual in my daily life. We kept quiet as we exited the lobby and he bumped my chair down the steps, but my mind raced on one repeat track: Do I give up or do I keep going? Give up or keep going?

FOR THE FOLLOW-UP medical exam requested by Dr. James, I brought support.

I wanted someone who was knowledgeable about disability and could act as a witness to the doctor's questions during the appointment, which would make me feel less vulnerable. I thought Dr. Theodore Childs, head of Long Island University's Disabled Students Program, an active member of the National Association for the Advancement of Colored People, and a World

War II veteran, would be perfect. He had firsthand experience with discrimination, was a kind and perceptive man who understood the situation, and, most of all, he was happy to help.

Again, Tony deftly backed my chair up the five steps. Again, Tony pushed the elevator button and walked with me and Dr. Childs to the doctor's office. Again, we sat and waited by the brown couch. But this time when the doctor poked her head into the small waiting room, there was no smile. And when I asked to bring Dr. Childs into the examining room, the doctor refused, insisting that he wait outside with Tony. My stomach dropped.

When I drove my wheelchair into the doctor's office, I saw two strange men already sitting in the room. Dr. James told me she had invited two other doctors to join in my medical exam.

With no introductions or any pretense of small talk, the three examined me together, firing a barrage of the same kinds of invasive questions: about my polio diagnosis, my medical history, my paralysis, and telling me, again, to walk for them. I had decided not to bring my crutches and braces. When I told the doctors this, I watched as Dr. James wrote something down.

Upside down on the form, I read her note: "Insubordinate."

At one point in the frenzied trial, Dr. James turned to the two men and said, "She wets her pants sometimes."

"What are you talking about?" I asked, incredulous.

Dr. James ignored me.

In the midst of the turmoil, I couldn't think straight. Words ran jaggedly through my body.

This cannot be happening, I thought. Cannot be . . . happening. No . . . not happening. No.

But the truth was, I just wanted to cry.

I was twenty-two years old and all I wanted to do was teach second graders.

Was there any training, any workshop, that could have prepared me for this?

What would you say to prepare someone for the fact that they would always be treated as an object of disease? As something less than human?

Three months later, the letter arrived in the mail: the New York City Board of Education had determined that I was unable to teach. It wasn't a surprise.

The reason: "Paralysis of both lower extremities, sequela of poliomyelitis."

I was officially considered a danger to children because I couldn't walk.

I wasn't contagious, but somehow I'd been deemed a contaminant.

It didn't matter how smart or capable I was, or how good my grades were, or how much experience I had. None of that mattered to the Board of Ed.

Because I couldn't walk, I wasn't considered qualified teach second graders.

They'd made their decision and printed it on the single sheet of white paper that had arrived in my mail.

CHAPTER 3

TO FIGHT OR NOT
TO FIGHT

I KNEW I HAD TO FIGHT THE BOARD OF ED, but I was insecure and uncertain what to do. This was the first time I was faced with making the decision to stand up for myself for the right to do something. Thinking about fighting for myself felt very different from when my parents had done it for me. I felt like I'd be put under a microscope and completely exposed, and I wasn't at all confident in my ability to actually teach. Could I really stand up and publicly demand the right to do something I'd never done before? Did I have the right? So many people would be watching me, wondering—could a woman in a wheelchair teach? What if I won this fight and then turned out to be a lousy teacher? I'd fail in front of everyone. If I wasn't successful at teaching, would people think that no one with a disability could teach? Would that ruin it for everyone? If there were thousands of us teaching, no one would notice one bad teacher, but if I was the only one and if I failed—what would that do to people's perception of disabled people? Thinking about it made me feel sick.

At the same time I felt responsible. My disabled friends rallied around me. We'd been expecting that I might be denied my license, and as soon as it happened my friends encouraged me to fight. We knew my case could be an example. It could raise awareness of our issues. I believed all this, but just because you believe something is right doesn't make it any easier to do. Knowing what I should do didn't mitigate the intense fear I felt in my body every time I thought about it.

But if I didn't fight, who would?

I called the ACLU back.

"I called you three years ago," I said and explained to the man on the phone what had happened since. I asked to make an appointment.

But the man told me I didn't need to come in.

"It's fine to just give us the information over the phone," he said. "Send whatever supporting documents you have. We'll assess it and call you back."

A few days later, he contacted me.

"I'm sorry, Miss Heumann. We've considered your case and determined that no discrimination has occurred. You've been denied your license for medical reasons, which is not discrimination."

I was speechless. How the doctor had treated me wasn't considered discriminatory? How could the denial of my teaching license on the grounds of my inability to walk *not* be discrimination? I was perfectly mobile in my wheelchair. I could even whisk children to safety on my lap if necessary. I'd passed all my exams, had done well in all my classes, and had far more hours of practical experience than required, with multiple age groups, as a result of the clinic Tony and I had developed.

For three years I'd been counting on the ACLU. Every time I'd gotten worried about what might happen when I went to get my license, I'd reminded myself that if things went south, the ACLU would help me. The civil rights movement was my inspiration. It had helped my disabled friends and me see that our barriers weren't our fault; they were a systemic problem. But now the ACLU was telling me it *was* my fault for having my disability. I was dumbfounded.

I racked my brain for a way to convince the ACLU representative. The problem was, I had no recourse. Disability wasn't covered at all in the Civil Rights Act of 1964. The Civil Rights Act was intended to end discrimination on the basis of race, color, religion, and national origin, but made no mention of disability. There was no law I could quote or legal precedent to cite. If I'd been covered under the Civil Rights Act, I could have hung up and called the Equal Opportunity Employment Commission, which had been created by the act. But there were no disability rights organizations. My only option was to try to persuade the man that discrimination against disabled people existed. I was so frustrated I wanted to cry. Instead, I forced myself to get very calm. He had to listen to me.

I tried again to explain.

"Please let me come in and talk with you," I said to the man. "I can explain how denying me my job on the grounds of medical condition is in fact discriminatory and you can't write it off as if I just failed the medical exam."

"I'm sorry, Miss Heumann. We've already assessed your case very thoroughly."

I was furious, and deep down I was very hurt.

Even the ACLU was a closed door to me.

Why was I constantly being forced to knock on doors where I wasn't welcome?

THE ACLU'S REACTION cemented my decision to fight. If even the ACLU couldn't understand how the Board of Ed's actions were discriminatory, then we had to blow my story up. We had to use my case to make it crystal clear that the barriers we faced to education, employment, transportation, to just living our lives, were not one-off problems. They were not medical problems to rehabilitate. We were not medical problems. I was never going to undo the damage polio had done to my nerve cells and walk again, nor was this my goal. The disabled veterans coming home from the Vietnam War were never going to grow their limbs back or heal their spinal cords and walk again. My friends with muscular dystrophy were never going to not have been born with muscular dystrophy. Accidents, illnesses, genetic conditions, neurological disorders, and aging are facts of the human condition, just as much as race or sex. So allowing schools and employers and city councils to design policies or buildings or buses in such a way that we couldn't participate was a violation of our civil rights. Which the government had a responsibility to protect.

But it wouldn't happen—the government would not take any responsibility—unless we made it impossible for them to ignore us.

The idea of bringing a lawsuit against the Board of Ed was daunting, and I had no clue how to do it. I didn't even know where to start. I definitely didn't know any lawyers. The people I knew were butchers and cops, teachers and firefighters. How did one go about finding a lawyer? How could I possibly find one who would see the Board of Education's decision as an issue of civil rights? If the ACLU didn't get it, what hope did I have of finding a mainstream lawyer who got it?

We decided we needed publicity. A disabled guy I knew from school was a journalism major and stringer for the *New York Times*. I called him and told him about the Board of Education's decision. The next day a reporter named Andrew Malcolm called to interview me. A week later, the article, "Woman in Wheel Chair Sues to Become Teacher," came out. It was 1970, and I was twenty-two years old.

I was at my apartment on Willoughby Street in Brooklyn. My roommate, Lori, picked up the paper for us.

"Judy! Judy!" She was waving the paper in front of her face. There was an article about my being denied the right to teach by the Board of Education. My mouth fell open. Although I'd been expecting it, the article blew me away. It was huge.

The next day, the *New York Times* wrote an editorial in support of my getting a job.

That afternoon I got a call. The man on the phone introduced himself as Roy Lucas. He was a lawyer with the James Madison Constitutional Law Center and informed me in a pleasant, understated kind of way that he'd read the article in the *Times* and would love to interview me for a project he was doing on civil rights.

Right away, I thought: A lawyer with knowledge of civil rights is calling me? It felt like a godsend. So while he was interviewing me, I decided to interview him. From the questions he asked and the way he spoke, I could tell he was intelligent and perceptive. At the end of the call, I asked if he would be willing to represent me as my lawyer. He agreed. Excitedly, I hung up the phone and cheered.

Roy Lucas's calling me out of the blue was like a miracle. It wasn't until much later that I learned just what a miracle it really was. Roy would go on to become one of America's most preeminent lawyers for abortion rights. In fairly short order, he would join the team who argued the monumental *Roe v. Wade* case before the Supreme Court, which legalized abortion in 1973. As a third-year law student at New York University, Roy had been the first person to articulate how constitutional privacy protection for married couples' use of birth control could be expanded into a legal argument for constitutional protection of a woman's right to an abortion—which was the foundation of the legal argument used in *Roe v. Wade*. Just six months before he called me, he had filed the first abortion rights lawsuit in New York. Roy would

couldn't be teachers—couldn't be whatever we decided we wanted to be.

It was at this time in my life that I first realized how energized I get by working together with people. When people recognize that they can't make change by themselves, that's when things really begin to happen. If you look at the people in my family, it's not that we've all been activists; it's that some of us have been able to find a strength within to fight for the things in life that not only benefit ourselves but also support all those around us.

After my appearance on *Today*, a number of things happened in quick succession. Roy called the Board of Education to verify their reason for the denial of my license, and on May 26, 1970, approximately three months after I had been denied my license, we filed my case in the Federal District Court. We were asking for the Board of Examiners' procedures to be judged as unconstitutional, my license to be granted, and $75,000 to be awarded to me in damages. In a story on May 27, the *New York Times* called the case "the first such civil rights suit ever filed in a Federal court," stating that the Board of Examiners had said they were "studying my appeal." The *Times* reporter wrote that members of both the Board of Education and the Board of Examiners felt "sorry for me, but that they had to assure the safety of pupils, such as during fire emergencies."

I was so tired of being called a fire hazard I could vomit.

But I was beginning to learn something very important: when institutions don't want to do something, to claim that something is a "safety" issue is an easy argument to fall back on. It sounds so benign and protective. How could caring about safety possibly be wrong or discriminatory? It's hard to argue against "safety." Everyone wants to feel safe; it's a basic human need.

"I have an electric wheelchair," I told the reporter. "It moves faster than people walking normally."

———————

IN NO TIME AT ALL, it was the day of the court hearing.

I drove my wheelchair into the courtroom flanked by my team of lawyers, with my parents and brothers trailing immediately behind. I positioned my chair in front of the judge's bench; Roy and Elias sat next to me. The bench was empty. Roy had told me that our judge was the first black female judge ever to be appointed to federal court. I was thrilled and couldn't wait to see her. Across the room from us, the lawyers and representatives from the school board were shuffling papers and whispering to each other. Next to them, a few reporters were already in the press section. Hearing the sound of motorized wheelchairs, I turned around and caught Frieda's eye as she wheeled into the room with a group of our friends. They smiled and waved. I was so filled with excited anticipation, I could barely hold still.

When the judge entered, those who could stand did so, and those of us in chairs sat up straighter. As she signaled for people to sit, I couldn't take my eyes off her. Judge Constance Baker Motley was tall and stately with carved cheekbones. But it wasn't her looks that captivated me, it was her presence. Her energy consumed the room. She was godlike.

Wow, wow, wow! This is amazing! was all I could think, over and over again. I thought back to my first phone call to the ACLU three and a half years ago; then I thought about how afraid I'd been to fight the Board of Education, the hurt and anger I'd felt after my last call to the ACLU.

The symbolism of the moment hit me. I was actually bringing a legal case against the New York City Board of Education and on the bench was the first black woman ever to be appointed a federal judge. The doors that had slid open unexpectedly to make this moment happen, combined with the serendipitous call from Roy Lucas, felt like fate.

It was very quick.

In a remarkably soft voice, Judge Baker Motley informed the representatives of the Board of Examiners and Board of Education that she was due for a change of bench, which meant a change of caseload, but that they should make no mistake about her interest in the case.

"I fully intend on keeping this case," she told them. "So I suggest that you do what you need to do to resolve this problem." With her concise words she made her meaning clear: do a review of this case, or else. With little argument, the representatives of the school district capitulated. They agreed to allow me to do another medical exam.

My third medical exam turned out to be completely inconsequential. I drove into the doctor's office and met the doctor, a younger woman. She basically sat at her desk, filled out some forms, and said, "I'm sorry. This never should have happened."

When it became unavoidably clear to the New York City Board of Education that they were losing, they settled out of court and I got my license.

WHEN I GOT OLDER, I learned how truly lucky I was to have had Constance Baker Motley as the judge on my case. At the time I had no idea of the role she'd played in the civil rights movement. The first black woman to graduate from Columbia Law School, Constance Baker Motley, in 1950, prepared the draft complaint for what would become *Brown v. Board of Education*. She was the only woman on the NAACP legal team for *Brown*. She'd also represented the freedom riders, who were integrating public transportation in the Deep South, and numerous plaintiffs who were integrating whites-only colleges. And she was the first black woman to be elected to the New York State Senate, after which she became the first black woman appointed to a federal court, which is when I met her.

I don't know if everything happens for a reason, but her presence felt like the result of otherworldly intervention. Many civil rights cases were assigned to federal judges who were vehemently antagonistic to the cause. With a different judge, my court case could have gone completely differently.

THE PERFECT ENDING TO THIS STORY about life-altering serendipitous moments would go something along the lines of "So then I got my license, found a job, and lived happily ever after." But that's not how it went, because I couldn't get a job, and then lots of other things happened.

After all the excitement of proving the Board of Education wrong in a very public court case, no one would hire me. Many of the schools were inaccessible and—I don't know if it was the result of the publicity or of discrimination, or of some combination of both—the response I got from many, many school principals was, "Well, I would have given you this job a few months ago, but given that there's such a short time frame, I don't have a position for you."

When the reporters who were following my story called me, I told them what was happening and a whole new round of editorials came out about my inability to get a job.

Eventually, the principal at my old school offered me a job, and I went back to P.S. 219. For the first year I didn't have my own class and mostly just taught whatever the teachers didn't want to do themselves. Finally, I ended up teaching both the disabled kids in Health Conservation 21 and the nondisabled kids in regular ed. For both the disabled and the nondisabled, it was the first time any of them had had a teacher with a disability. After that first year, I got my own class and went on to teach for two more years.

During the whole year of the court case and my first teaching job, articles about me and my cause continued to appear—at least one article a month. Many people recognized me and stopped me on the street. People in their car driving down the street would stop to honk their horns, so I would go over and say hello. They came up to me in stores and stopped me walking down the sidewalk. Some of them just would just say, "Congratulations! Keep it up." But others told me yet more stories about problems of discrimination.

When I think back, I am in awe at how differently things could have gone if I had given in to my fear and insecurity. What if I'd just let the issue go because I didn't want to make a fuss? To begin with, I never would have known whether I was able to teach. Even more important, I would have been accepting what the system was telling me about who I was and what I could do. Even if I'd lost the court case, just bringing the case would still have changed my life because I stood up and told the system that it was wrong about me. I was fighting for what I believed in.

The fact that I did win validated my perspective on our issues, which was that people with disabilities do face discrimination, and if we take the time to fight, we may win.

Later, the State of New York passed legislation to ensure that people who are blind or physically disabled are not prevented from teaching.

The other thing that happened in the aftermath of the court case was that my friends and I decided to organize a civil rights organization: an organization run by and for disabled people.

We reached out to all the people who had written to me or called me and invited them to our first meeting, which we held at LIU. More than a hundred people showed up, including some press. Given that there was no accessible public transportation, this was a phenomenal showing of interest. At first we called the new organization Handicapped in Action, but in fairly short order we changed the name to Disabled in Action, since we disliked the term "handicapped." I was elected the fledgling organization's first president, and the board of directors was made up of people with all types of disabilities. We worked on a whole slate of issues, from ending sheltered workshops and institutionalization to fighting for accessible transportation and protesting against the *New York Times* for their failure to cover disability-related news as a civil rights issue. We worked with other organizations, such as the Willowbrook State School, a hellhole institution on Staten Island that housed thousands of people with developmental disabilities, and we teamed up with disabled vets coming back from Vietnam.

When other people see you as a third-class citizen, the first thing you need is a belief in yourself and the knowledge that you have rights.

The next thing you need is a group of friends to fight back with.

CHAPTER 4

FEAR OF FLYING

I WAS SITTING at my desk in my bedroom on Willoughby Street in Brooklyn. Spread out in front of me were pages and pages of legislation that Congress had proposed as amendments to the proposed Rehabilitation Act. It was 1972 and I was twenty-five. I was spending my weekend off from teaching wading through policies. A friend, Eunice Fiorito, who was director of the New York City Mayor's Office for People with Disabilities, had called to tell me about the new legislation that related to supporting disabled people in education, training, and entering the workforce. As you may recall, the US Office of Vocational Rehabilitation, Rehab for short, had financially supported my education at LIU; it was important to those of us with disabilities and we had a lot of concerns about how the program was run. Eunice, who was blind, had at first had one of her staff read the language to me over the phone, but then she couriered it over to me so I could go through it on the weekend.

I was sipping a cup of water, moving slowly through the language about training and services, when I read the sentence in Section 504.

"Wait, wait a minute." I put my tea down. "Did I read that right?"

I read the sentence over again, took my glasses off, rubbed my eyes, and read the sentence one more time.

I *was* reading correctly. I couldn't believe it. I stared at the paper, reading the sentence over and over again:

> No otherwise qualified handicapped individual in the United States, as defined in section 7(6), shall, solely by reason of his handicap, be excluded from the participation in, be denied the benefits of, or be subjected to discrimination under any program or activity receiving Federal financial assistance.

This sentence acknowledged that the way we were being treated *was actually discrimination*.

My mind churned, processing.

Someone in Congress finally understood what we'd been saying: that our being denied entrance to school, or teaching credentials, or any of the thousands of other barriers we regularly hit, could not, *should not*, be dismissed as medical issues.

Excitement started to bubble up inside me.

There were people in Congress who not only were learning about what we were facing, but were willing to take action. The enormity of what this could mean hit me, and I paused, reflecting.

What if I had never had to experience being denied entry into school? What if I'd never had all this self-doubt planted in my brain?

From some buried place inside me, tiny tendrils of confusion, hurt, and shame loosened, rising to the surface—the feelings that lingered from my childhood, that came from never being able to understand *why*. Why *couldn't* I go to school with my brother and my friends? It had never made sense to me.

This was the why. This discrimination, that people always insisted didn't exist, that people tried to wash away by saying they didn't mean it, they didn't understand, they didn't know what to do.

I began to envision what the law could look like. It only covered entities receiving money from the federal government—but that could include so much of what we'd been facing in education, some forms of employment, housing, transportation.

Disabled in Action and our partner organizations—we could work on this. The fight was moving forward.

We were finally being heard.

Back in 1964, when the Civil Rights Act had been passed and even before, when it had only been proposed, there had been announcements, speeches, and articles heralding the process and the achievement. You would think that, as civil rights legislation for disability, Section 504 would have similar excitement around it. But I'd heard nothing about this proposed Rehabilitation Act having any civil rights provisions in it. As far as I knew, no one had talked about this bill as civil rights legislation in any way, shape, or form. Perhaps this should have surprised me, but at the time it didn't. I was so used to our issues getting ignored that my expectations were very low. Later I would learn that Section 504 was the stealthy work of a few of our champion senators who'd asked some of their senior staff to figure out how to quietly insert civil rights provisions into a bill primarily focused on employment for disabled people—without having to amend the Civil Rights Act.

Once I'd fully processed what I'd read, I started to call members of the DIA board of directors to discuss what to do. At that time there were only about eighty of us, but we were very active. We had a committee structure and specific goals related to ending sheltered workshops, increasing accessibility, and fighting the negative representation of disability on television. We started tracking the bill. Regardless of how Section 504 had come about, we weren't going to let it go.

Congress voted to pass the bill, but President Nixon exercised his right to veto it by letting it sit on his desk without signing it into law. To call attention to the veto, we decided to hold a demonstration. Nixon was running for reelection, so he was a good target. Our protest started with about fifty of us going to a federal building in Manhattan. Unfortunately, there was very little happening in the area. No one paid any attention to us, except the police, who showed up and asked us what we wanted. We asked them if they knew where the Nixon campaign headquarters was and they gave us the address, which, it turned out, was on Madison Avenue, a main thoroughfare in the city. So we rolled over there and wheeled ourselves into the middle of Madison Avenue, shutting down all four lanes, the trucks and cars honking and blaring at us. But it was rush hour—we'd met our match. So we decided to just block one lane of traffic, and that was enough to cause a major traffic jam. Although we got no press coverage, we did get reported on in the evening traffic report.

We decided we would have another protest the day before the presidentital election.

Looking to recruit some Vietnam vets to join us, we connected with Bobby Muller, who had started Vietnam Veterans of America and was a paraplegic.

"I've finally met someone crazier than me," he said to me as we marched through Times Square to Nixon's headquarters. Because veterans were young, male, and historically regarded as heroes, the government viewed them differently from us. We hoped that having a few disabled veterans join our protest would improve press coverage, and it did, a little.

That was my life for the years after I got my teaching license. During the week, I taught and did what I could for Disabled in Action. On the weekends we had meetings, organized, and protested.

I WAS AT HOME ONE DAY when the phone rang. I picked it up in the kitchen, where I had a yellow phone mounted on the wall. It was early afternoon and the sun was shining into the dining room and kitchen. I was twenty-seven.

"Judy," the man said, as if calling me was something he did every day, "this is Ed Roberts. I am calling from Berkeley, California. I've heard a lot about you. I want you to move here, to Berkeley. I think, together, we could really make a difference."

"Wait. What? Why?" I was surprised, but I was smiling. It felt good to be wanted. But who was this person? I laughed. This was like something I would do—call someone out of the blue to ask them to do something totally unexpected. Although I had never asked someone to move across the country, at least not yet.

"I've heard about what you're doing with Disabled in Action in New York," Ed said. "Public Health and City and Regional Planning at [the University of California at] Berkeley are looking for students with disabilities. I imagine you're more than qualified."

He continued: "And my goal is for you to get involved with the Center for Independent Living. I'm recruiting leaders who can be a part of what we're doing."

I had vaguely heard of the Center for Independent Living.

"Mmmm," I said.

The Center for Independent Living (CIL) was the first of its kind in the world, Ed explained. Like Disabled in Action, it was focused on empowerment but it combined its work with policies and services that allowed disabled people to live independently. Ed had had polio, he went on to tell me, and could use only two fingers. He slept in an iron lung and used a motorized wheelchair. He'd been the first person with a significant disability to attend the University of California, Berkeley, and he'd had to fight the university administration to be allowed to live on campus. Because there were no buildings designed to support the weight of his iron lung, he'd had to live in an empty wing of the university hospital. Pretty quickly, though, other disabled students in wheelchairs had come to Berkeley and moved into his "dorm." They called themselves the Rolling Quads and founded the Physically Disabled Students Program at Berkeley. The Center for Independent Living, which Ed was the director of, had grown out of the Physically Disabled Students Program at Berkeley. It was mainly made up of young disabled activists.

I was immediately intrigued by the idea of getting my master's at Berkeley and by the sound of the Center for Independent Living. As a teacher I was required to get my master's. I'd already been accepted to Columbia University, but I'd been trying to figure out how I was going to commute from Brooklyn to uptown Manhattan. But the prospect of leaving New York frightened me. Between the support of my family and paying my roommates to help me get up and dressed, go to bed at night, and go to the bathroom, I'd cobbled together a support system that allowed me to live in my own apartment. The thought of leaving my support system made me feel like I could fall into a deep hole.

I told Ed I didn't think I could leave New York—I wasn't sure I wanted to leave my family and I definitely didn't want to leave the supports I'd built.

"Judy, this is exactly the point of what we're doing out here." Then he told me about everything he was able to do independently in Berkeley. The State of California provided financial support for disabled people to hire personal assistance, so they didn't have to be dependent on roommates and friends, as I was in New York. And the Center for Independent Living represented a community that could help me figure out how to access everything I needed to be on my own—like how to find an accessible apartment, where to repair my wheelchair if necessary, and how to actually advertise for and hire a personal assistant, which I'd never done before. Listening to Ed, I began to imagine it might be possible to move. Gradually, my fear started to dissipate.

I told him I would think about it.

I hung up. Could I actually do this? I talked about the call with my parents and friends, and thought about all the possible implications. It would be a huge change for me. Not only would I be leaving Disabled in Action and all of my friends and family, but I'd be leaving my wonderful voice teacher. I'd been studying voice with him for ten years, and the idea of leaving him felt very emotional.

In the end I decided to apply to the program and was accepted to the master's program in public health at UC Berkeley, which in turn triggered my getting accepted by the Department of Rehabilitation as a client—they would pay for my graduate program. I told my friend Nancy D'Angelo about what I was thinking. She got excited about moving, too, so we decided to go together. I don't know whether I would have done it if we hadn't decided to move together.

WHEN WE ARRIVED IN CALIFORNIA, Ed and some of the staff at Center for Independent Living, as well as people from the Disabled Students' Program at Berkeley, helped us. They found us an apartment and had someone meet us at the airport who could help us for our first few days in California. Once we were deemed eligible for in-home assistance, we identified and found our own support. Personal-assistant work was respected in Berkeley, and it wasn't difficult to find people. It was a strange and amazing feeling to be able to interview and hire people whose explicit job was to help me in the specific ways and at the specific times I needed it. I hired someone to come in the morning and the evening, and then I had someone to act as backup if my regular person didn't show up on a Friday or Saturday night. As a result, I got to decide when I wanted to get up, when and what I wanted to eat, and when I wanted to go to sleep. I could go out on Saturday nights without worrying about how I'd get to bed! The fact that Berkeley was a small, compact city gave me the freedom to move around by myself. Without having to depend on my brother or my father to drive me, I could get to my friends' houses by myself. For the first time, I had friends with wheelchair-accessible vans, like Ed.

The Center for Independent Living was in our apartment building and it was a hotbed of people and activity. Folks were coming to California from all over the country to be a part of the movement that was growing there. Other people followed us from New York. Suddenly, I was socializing up a storm in a way that I'd never known before. I don't think I can overstate how much I, a true extrovert, loved this. I joined the Center for Independent Living board of directors, got involved in the Disabled Students' Program at Berkeley, and immersed myself in the disabled activist community.

On the Berkeley campus, I was the only student in my master's program with a visible disability. So how did I fit in, you might be wondering? Well, fabulously.

My work with my adviser, Professor Henrik Blum, made me feel that my ideas and goals for disabled people were perfectly rational. He agreed with the concept that health and quality of life could not just be about medical care, but needed to include the vast array of needs required to lead a healthy life—accessibility, housing, education, employment. Professor Blum recommended me to serve on the board of directors of the Over 60s Health Clinic, which was much more than a health clinic. One of my contributions to the board was to introduce the idea that disability was a natural part of the aging process; thus, the fact that people acquire disabilities as they age should be accommodated, so people can remain active in the community. There were, unfortunately, no accessible bathrooms in Warren Hall, the building where I spent most of my time, so to go to the toilet I had to go clear across campus to get assistance at the Disabled Students'

Program, which was a hassle and took a chunk of time out of my day. But I loved the ease with which I could get across the Berkeley campus, and I loved the students I met and learned from in class.

I'D BEEN IN BERKELEY for less than a year when my phone rang again. I was in my kitchen looking into our back garden.

"Judy, this is Lisa Walker," said the voice on the other end of the line. "I'm the senior legislative person for Senator Harrison Williams. I'd like to talk with you about a job in our office."

I wasn't surprised to be hearing from Lisa. Ralf Hotchkiss, a friend from DC who worked for Ralph Nader, had called me a few weeks before to ask if he could recommend me for a legislative assistant position in Senator Williams's office. I'd been looking for a six-month placement to fulfill the practicum prerequisite for my master's. This was a full-time position, but if Berkeley was willing to let me complete my degree from a distance, I thought it sounded like a great opportunity. So I'd said yes, I'd be interested.

Lisa invited me to apply.

My mind flip-flopped.

On Capitol Hill, Senator Williams was one of the congressional champions of disability issues. As chair of the Senate Committee on Labor and Public Welfare, he was in a position to make a substantial difference on employment and education for people with disabilities, two issues obviously very close to my heart. On the other hand, I loved my life in Berkeley, although—interestingly—I didn't feel the same fear about leaving Berkeley to move to Washington as I'd felt about leaving New York. The move to California had boosted my confidence in my ability to live independently.

I applied, and in fairly short order I got the job. I moved again.

MY LIFE IN WASHINGTON was more restricted than it had been in Berkeley. There were no personal-assistant referral programs in DC, like the one CIL had developed in Berkeley, and it was very difficult to find personal assistants. In addition, getting around the city was much more challenging, since there was no accessible public transit, although the California Department of Rehabilitation made my move possible by paying for my transportation to and from work, allowing me to hire a van and a driver. Because of the lack of accessibility and personal assistance, I had less ability to socialize, but luckily I moved in with a friend, Diane Latin, a paraplegic who worked for the President's Committee on Employment of the Handicapped. I had the bedroom and she slept on the couch in the living room. Smart and outspoken, Diane had long, flaming-red hair. She was way wilder than me and I loved it. We had the same vision for what we wanted the future to look like for disabled people.

On Capitol Hill I worked closely with Lisa Walker, as well as with Nik Edes, who was a high-level staff person for the Senate Committee on Labor and Public Welfare. Lisa and Nik were two of the congressional staffers who played a big role in supporting people with disabilities, which is one of the reasons Lisa had reached out to me. They wanted to strengthen their relationship with activists.

Senator Williams's office gave me a position on the team working on Section 504, which I had not stopped tracking since the day I'd first read that short paragraph. The Rehabilitation Act, including Section 504, had been finally signed by Nixon while I was in California. Incidentally, I arrived in DC just as the Watergate scandal was peaking, and Nixon resigned not long after I got there. That had many implications for Section 504, because it meant we now had a whole new administration to lobby and bring up to speed. The law would have no teeth without enabling regulations that would instruct the other federal agencies and institutions how Section 504 was to be interpreted and enforced. So the next step was for President Gerald Ford's incoming administration to write the enabling regulations. That job fell to the Department of Health, Education, and Welfare, otherwise known as HEW. Sitting through various committee meetings, I came to understand this fact very clearly.

Senator Williams's office was also involved in other major issues and legislation. One issue on the table was how to make sure disabled children got a quality education. I was asked for my input. What? You mean I can use my wounding childhood experiences to help design laws that will change kids' lives? It was exciting. I was diplomatic, but I didn't hold back.

"Close down special-ed schools and get disabled students into regular classrooms!" I advocated. "What can we do to make sure that disabled students will actually be expected to learn?" I was smack in the middle of the action and it was becoming increasingly clear that my background and activism gave me knowledge and expertise that others didn't have.

I played a role in helping to develop the Education for All Handicapped Children's Act legislation that would eventually become the Individuals with Disabilities Education Act (known as IDEA), ensuring that disabled children are learning in the least restrictive environment possible, shutting down segregated schools, and creating accountability for delivering quality education to disabled students. Of course I was also doing a lot of the kind of daily grunt work you do in those jobs, such as answering letters and prepping materials. But my thoughts and opinions were being valued, and this shifted the ground beneath my feet.

I met people from a wide range of disability organizations: organizations for those with cerebral palsy or muscular dystrophy, and also for deaf people, blind, cognitively disabled, and more. I connected with staffers, activists, and lobbyists, all kinds of people I'd never met before. It was fertile ground for starting things. I helped cofound the American Coalition of Citizens with Disabilities as a mechanism for tracking Section 504 and making sure it was implemented in a way that worked for us. This became the first national cross-disability rights organization run by and for people with disabilities.

It was during that time that the incident on the plane happened.

It was a cold gray day in January and I was at LaGuardia Airport in Queens, waiting for my flight back to DC. I'd been home for the holidays. My parents were waiting with me, to help me get on the plane and to say goodbye. I was feeling a little blue about leaving my parents and was not excited about the flight. I didn't like flying. To make myself feel better, I'd brought Erica Jong's book *Fear of Flying* to read on the plane. It had come out just two years earlier, in 1973. Rolling to the door of the gate, I dug my ticket out of my bag. As I went to hand it to the woman at the counter, however, she paused.

"Who are you flying with today?" she asked me.

I looked at her, annoyed.

"No one. I'm flying by myself."

"I'm sorry, ma'am, but you're not allowed to fly by yourself," she said, a bit dismissively.

Now, I knew for a fact that there actually were no regulations in place prohibiting anyone with a disability from flying. At that very moment, in the bag on my lap, I happened to have a copy of the Department of Transportation's newly proposed regulations, which were on my to-do list to review for our office. Since I'd already read them, I knew that they proposed to restrict travel for people like me to fly independently, a provision our office didn't support. So I was very aware that these restrictions did not exist in the current regulations.

I asked to speak with her supervisor and she called another woman over, who immediately sided with her. So I asked to speak with that person's supervisor. Eventually a man showed up and told me I could board the plane.

Under the regulations in force at that time, my father was allowed to board the plane to help me into the seat, which he now did. Although I had been forceful with the women at the gate, I was feeling a little shaken. Whenever these incidents occurred—whether in a movie theater where I was told that I was blocking the aisle, or in a restaurant where the manager clearly wished we weren't there—I tended to be strong in the moment but always left feeling upset and angry. I took out my book and tried to calm myself down.

We were waiting for takeoff when the pilot came on to the intercom and announced that the flight was on hold—not cleared for takeoff.

A flight attendant walked toward me. It looked like I might be the reason we were on hold.

"I'm sorry, ma'am, you're not permitted to fly by yourself. If you don't have someone who can be with you to help you in the event of an emergency, then I'm going to have to ask you to get off the plane."

I smiled at the flight attendant.

"In the event of an emergency," I informed her, "I am not going to be the only person who needs help off the plane." The flight attendant's smile tightened. She turned to the man next to me.

"Sir, would you be willing to help this woman in the event of an emergency?" The guy agreed to help me. But I intervened.

"No, thank you," I said to the man. "In the event of an emergency, I am sure they'll need to be dealing with the situation and helping more people than me. I am not unique." The smile left the flight attendant's face.

"Ma'am, we are going to have to have a doctor come on the plane to certify that you can travel on your own." People around us turned their heads to look at me.

"Well," I said calmly, "if you're planning on doing a medical exam for everyone on the plane, that's fine with me." By this time, the flight attendant had been joined by a small group of other attendants, who clustered around her. One of them pushed forward to speak to me.

"I'm sorry, ma'am, you're going to have to get off the plane."

"No," I said firmly, emphatically. "I will not get off the plane." The entire plane full of passengers was looking at me.

The flight attendants turned around. One walked off the plane and the rest gathered around the cabin door, whispering.

A few minutes later, two Port Authority policemen boarded the plane. They walked directly to my seat.

"Ma'am, you're under arrest. Please leave your seat." They looked and sounded very serious. But all I could think was, Wow!! This is amazing! Finally, they're going to arrest me and we'll be able to do something with this to show another example of discrimination!

So they took me off the plane. Once we were in the airport, they asked for my ID. I didn't have a regular ID because I didn't drive, so I gave them my credit card—which was new, by the way, since women couldn't apply for their own credit in the US until that very year, 1975. When they said that wasn't good enough, I gave them my Senate ID card. As soon as they saw my Senate ID, they paused.

"You work in the Senate?"

"Yes, I do." They exchanged a glance.

"Who do you work for?"

"Senator Harrison Williams." Their faces shifted; they no longer looked threatening.

"Harrison Williams from New Jersey?"

"Yes."

They were Port Authority police, which meant they worked for both the State of New York and the State of New Jersey.

"Well, ma'am, we're going to let you go this time."

I knew it! I thought. Now here I was at the airport, they've made me miss the last flight out, and they were too chicken to even arrest me! I decided to call my friend Malachy McCourt, who had a radio show in New York. He and his wife, Diane, have a daughter with a disability and were very active on disability rights. Maybe I could at least get some press out of this. The next day, thanks to Malachy, a newspaper story came out about what had happened.

I brought a case against the airlines. When we went to court, the judge said I had a history of being litigious and I'd set everything up intentionally. He basically threw the case out, saying it wasn't discrimination. Of course I had no recourse. We appealed, but the case was remanded back to the first judge. He said that the case wasn't worth more than $500, although at the end of the day we settled out of court for a lot more.

ABOUT A YEAR AND A HALF into my time in DC, my phone rang yet again. It was Ed.

"Judy, Governor Jerry Brown has offered me the position of head of [the Department of] Rehabilitation for the State of California," he told me. "Would you consider coming back to Berkeley to take on the deputy director role at the Center for Independent Living?"

I moved back to Berkeley. I was still young, only twenty-seven.

It was good to be back in Berkeley. In my new position at the Center for Independent Living, I found that my time in DC had given my activism a gigantic leg up. I had new information, new relationships, and new ideas for strategy.

Section 504 was still very much on our radar. President Ford's department of Health, Education, and Welfare had drafted the enabling regulations and then issued them for comment. The organization we'd cofounded in DC, the American Coalition of

Citizens with Disabilities, mobilized support, provided comments, and gave feedback. The Handicapped Lobby, reporters called us. Institutions around the country did the same.

To finalize the regulations, all that was needed was the signature of Ford's secretary of Health, Education, and Welfare, David Matthews. But he was delaying.

The problem was that the stealthy way Section 504 had come about meant that none of the universities, hospitals, or other institutions that would be affected by the regulations had really paid attention to it until the Ford administration had issued the draft regulations for comment. Then, when they'd read them and begun to understand the implications, they were not happy. In general, institutions don't like change because change takes time and can entail costs. In particular, the institutions didn't see the need for spending resources to adapt their buildings, programs, or classrooms for disabled people. It would be too costly, they argued, an unfair financial burden—and how many disabled people really went to university, or participated in x, y, or z specific activity, anyway?

Right there was our catch-22: Because the country was so inaccessible, disabled people had a hard time getting out and doing things—which made us invisible. So we were easy to discount and ignore. Until institutions were forced to accommodate us we would remain locked out and invisible—and as long as we were locked out and invisible, no one would see our true force and would dismiss us.

The institutions had their lobbyists put the pressure on to try to break down the potential impact of Section 504. And, as can happen, the government was caving in to the pressure of those with clout by delaying.

We were rallying support, lobbying back, and at one point we brought a lawsuit against the government.

Still, nothing we did was big enough or strong enough to exceed the power of the institutions and push the government into signing.

By late 1976 and the election of Jimmy Carter, the regulations were still unsigned.

Once again we were dealing with a new administration. During his campaign, Jimmy Carter had promised that *his* HEW secretary would sign the regulations drafted by Ford's administration. We stepped up our efforts.

But as of April 1977, it appeared that Carter's new secretary of HEW, Joseph Califano, had no intention of signing the regulations either.

PART TWO

BERKELEY, CALIFORNIA

1977

CHAPTER 5

DETAINED

I PICKED SOME underwear out of my drawer and handed it and my toothbrush to my personal assistant, Carol.

"Do you mind putting these in my bag for me?" I turned my wheelchair around so she could reach the black backpack hanging there. Carol was used to my morning routine; she came every morning to help me get from my bed to my wheelchair, bathe, go to the bathroom, put a little makeup on, and get dressed.

"Going somewhere?" Carol asked me casually, as she packed my toothbrush and underwear into my backpack. She knew I didn't normally pack an extra set of undergarments for a day at the office. As the deputy director of the Center for Independent Living, I did travel a lot, it was true. I was often in DC as well as speaking all over the country, but Carol knew I wasn't scheduled to leave town.

Carol and I had a good relationship. We were as friendly as any two people who shared such an intimate part of the day. But that day I kept my distance.

"The rally may go a little long today," I said lightly, putting on my big silver rimmed glasses as she zipped my jacket. If things went as we thought they might, there was a chance I might not return home for several days.

I could get detained.

I said goodbye to Carol and drove my wheelchair onto the sidewalk in front of my house. Feeling the chill of a normal Berkeley morning, I looked up and down the street. The plan was for Paul, a staff person from CIL, to pick me up in a van, but I was a little early. I took advantage of the time alone to collect my thoughts.

At our last American Coalition of Citizens with Disabilities board meeting, Eunice Fiorito, who had become the president of the board, and Frank Bowe, our newly hired executive director, who was deaf, had reported on their concerns about Califano's lack of progress on signing the regulations. We were all very frustrated. We knew that the longer Califano delayed, the more likely it was that changes would be made to water down the regulations. We had to up the pressure on Califano to sign. So we passed a motion stating that if the regulations were not signed as they'd be written under the Ford Administration by April 5, there would be demonstrations around the country.

Then we'd made a public announcement, giving HEW advance warning.

Today was April 5.

We had targeted ten HEW offices across the country: the national office, in Washington, DC, and nine regional offices in Atlanta, Boston, New York City, Los Angeles, Denver, Chicago, Dallas, Philadelphia, and San Francisco.

I was charged with planning the San Francisco demonstration, which made the Center for Independent Living the lead organization. The first thing we did was create a committee to organize it. The Committee to Save 504, we called it, and Kitty Cone was asked to lead it. Kitty, who had muscular dystrophy and used a wheelchair, was a community organizer extraordinaire. In college at the University of Illinois, she'd joined the antiwar movement and, much to the chagrin of her upper-crust family, had become a Trotskyite. At CIL, Kitty was a staff person working in community affairs. She and I worked very closely together on the Section 504 protest.

By that time CIL had been building a power base for years—recruiting activists, creating alliances with other civil rights groups by supporting their rallies and causes, launching successful campaigns for personal assistance, advocating for accessible transportation, and working with Ed on expanding the number of CILs across the country. Organizing for April 5 was a natural extension of what we'd already been doing. As we planned for the demonstration, however, Kitty and I started to worry. Both of us had had the experience of being ignored many times in our lives. We knew how it worked. The government could be very good at placating and pretending to be acting, when they were actually just stalling until the public eye got distracted. Kitty and I were hell-bent that we would not let this happen in this situation. It was an "over my dead body" kind of thing to us. So, quietly, we had decided to take our protest one step further.

Which is why I had an extra set of undies in my backpack.

"HEY! HOW'S IT GOING? Ready?"

I'd been so lost in my thoughts I hadn't noticed Paul pulling up in the CIL van. He hopped out and came around the side of the van to where I was parked on the sidewalk.

"Ready as I'll ever be," I said.

I wheeled myself onto the van's lift while Paul got back into the driver's seat and pushed the button to activate the lift. We drove down Ashby Street.

"Looks like it's going to be good weather today," I commented, as we pulled onto the freeway. Paul nodded, focused on navigating converging lanes of cars. The van sped south, toward Oakland and the Bay Bridge.

As the van crossed the Bay Bridge, the buildings of San Francisco emerged from the clouds. Paul took the second exit off the bridge, and suddenly, we were in the middle of the city. All around us people were walking down the sidewalk, chatting, waiting at traffic lights, crossing streets—stepping up, down, and over the curbs, without even noticing what they were doing. Sometimes I marveled at the ease with which other people navigated curbs like they were nothing, whereas, to me, a simple twelve-inch curb was a complete dead end.

Paul pulled the van into a parking spot across the street from the San Francisco Federal Building, at 50 United Nations Plaza. It housed most of the federal agencies in the city; without question, the imposing six-story granite building was impressive. Built in the beaux arts style, it was a monumental piece of architecture, rich with sculptural detailing. The front of the building faced a large pedestrian plaza, where three ornate archways curved over the main entrance.

Prep for the demonstration was already in motion, and the team from CIL was in full swing. Dead center in front of the building sat Kitty in her wheelchair, instructing a group of men as they assembled a temporary stage. As she wheeled around and shouted orders, even from a distance I could see her face glowing with excitement under her brown curly hair.

Kitty had organized a structure for the demonstration. People were charged with heading various committees for outreach and media, and everything else we would need for the day. Mary Jane Owen, who had low vision, had helped handle the outreach. Kitty had given Mary Jane a long list of organizations to call for endorsements, and bundles of posters to distribute. Then it was up to Mary Jane to do the arduous work of calling each group, to ask, "Would you hand out some leaflets? Would you notify your membership?" Kitty had called the press herself. Steve McClel-

land, who was deaf, had lined up the sign language interpreters
and sound equipment. Another group of people had worked on
logistics for the rally.

As I watched, two men took a microphone and sound system out of the back of a van to where another was setting up
a table. I could see Steve McClelland supervising, speaking in
sign language with the sound guys. Joe Quinn, the sign language
interpreter, stood next to Steve, speaking in chorus with Steve's
rapidly moving hands. Joe was hard to miss, with his tall frame
and handlebar mustache. Ten or so other people hurried back
and forth across the plaza, carrying things, setting things up, and
talking. A couple of people walked with white canes, another
spoke in sign language with an interpreter, and the rest were
in wheelchairs. Walking with Mary Jane was my boyfriend, Jim
Pechin, with wavy dark hair, wearing his aviator sunglasses.

I'd come a long way from my lonely dateless nights in the
dorm at LIU. In the four years since I'd first moved to Berkeley
from New York, I'd happily discovered that I was actually considered quite attractive. With little hesitation, I'd joined the sexual
revolution and gone out with a number of men. Jim was a veteran who'd spent fourteen months as a helicopter gun door gun-
ner in Vietnam. He'd started to question the war on every level
and since coming home had become very active in the antiwar
movement. Hundreds of thousands of vets had come back from
Vietnam disabled, and Jim had cofounded Swords to Plough-
shares to support them and had been hired as the coordinator of
the new CIL paralegal program. At that time Jim wasn't disabled,
although he would later develop diabetes and other health issues
related to Agent Orange exposure.

Catching sight of me from across the plaza, Kitty smiled and
beckoned for me to come over. As I drove toward her, a group
of people rounded the corner of the building, and six others in

wheelchairs poured from a van parked on the street. Some of them were clutching the leaflets Kitty and I had made a week or so ago. We'd been sitting at the kitchen table in my apartment, late at night, trying to come up with a slogan for the demonstration. We needed something short and catchy. Kitty had an X-Acto knife that she was using to cut little plastic letters out of a mold. But how do you boil a complex issue down into a few words that will get people to come out and protest? We were totally cracking up, just losing it. Is this how change actually happens? Does everything start at someone's kitchen table, brainstorming slogans at midnight, cutting rickety little plastic letters out of a mold?

Finally we composed ourselves enough to come up with "People with Disabilities: The Federal Government Is Trying to Steal Our Civil Rights!"

Amazingly, it looked like our slogan actually worked, I thought, as the plaza started to fill up around me.

It was a perfect sunny day. I was in my jacket, but most people were in short sleeves, the sun on their faces.

Later, sitting on the stage listening to the speakers, I was excited about the size of the crowd. I estimated that there were two, maybe three hundred people. I was quite happy to see we had a cross section of disability and a good degree of racial representation. The Reverend Cecil Williams, who was African American and the cofounder of Glide Memorial Church, had spoken first and the other speakers were following one by one: Tom Hayden, a civil rights leader who would later become a congressman; feminist Sylvia Bernstein; a representative from the Black Panthers—each building on the energy of the next. I loved that our work supporting the causes of African Americans, feminists, unions, the gay community, and other civil rights groups was paying off, and they were now supporting us in return. The crowd was rowdy, applauding uproariously after each speaker—the hearing people clapping, the deaf people raising their hands and shaking them in front of their faces. Joe Quinn was standing next to the speaker on the stage, his hands signing.

Wheelchair positioned in front of the microphone, Kitty was just finishing her speech. She launched into a chant. "Sign 504! Sign 504 unchanged! Sign 504 unchanged!" The crowd, which seemed to be growing, clapped and chanted, the deaf people signing in unison.

It was my turn to speak.

I drove my chair forward to the microphone, a "Sign 504" sticker on my jacket, my heart pounding.

The crowd cheered. I sat a moment and waited for quiet.

Hundreds of faces looked expectantly at me.

I began.

"When I was five years old, I was denied the right to school because the school wasn't accessible. When I was finally allowed to start school in the fourth grade, some of my classmates were eighteen years old and still didn't know how to read.

"When they are signed, the regulations for Section 504 will be an historic and monumental first step toward knocking down the walls that stop us, people with disabilities, from being full and equal participants in society.

"For the past few years"—I choked up, paused and looked down; the crowd was utterly silent—"we have played by the rules." I took a breath, trying to get ahold of myself. "We created the American Coalition of Citizens with Disabilities. We attended meetings in Washington, commented on drafts, and spoke with institutions all over the country. We were told Jimmy Carter's administration would sign the regulations, unchanged. We believed him.

"Now Secretary Califano is dragging his feet. We have no reason to trust him. We are here to say enough is enough.

"For too long, we have believed that if we played by the rules and did what we were told, we would be included in the American Dream.

"We have waited too long, made too many compromises, and been too patient.

"We will no longer be patient. There will be no more compromise.

"We will accept no more discrimination."

I stopped speaking. For a split second I gazed out at the crowd and then raised my hand and chanted.

"Sign 504! Sign 504! Unchanged! Sign 504 unchanged!"

The crowd thundered, chanting, shouting, raising their hands, shaking them, and cheering. I chanted with them for a minute and then turned to wheel to the back of the stage. Ed Roberts was already behind me.

"That was great," he said and grinned.

I grinned back.

Now it was Ed's turn at the microphone. From his reclining wheelchair, he spoke, the assistant holding the microphone in front of his face. This is what I recall Ed saying: "When I was fourteen I had polio. While I was sick the doctor said to my mother, 'You should hope he dies because if he survives he will be a vegetable.'

"When I recovered, my life had changed. For a long time I wanted to die. I stopped eating to try and kill myself. And then I realized I didn't want to die." Ed looked handsome as the breeze ruffled his brown hair. He was out of his iron lung and using his "frog" breathing technique, gulping air into his lungs after every few words. Next to him stood Joe Quinn, his hands moving.

"So I come before you now as an artichoke, prickly on the outside with a big heart on the inside," he said.

"When you see me, I hope that you see what is possible, where others saw only what was not possible.

"And I tell you this. Our whole lives we are told what we can and cannot do. But know this now: what we are trying to do here is possible.

"Only we decide what is right for us."

The whole plaza was hanging on his every word.

"So, WHAT DO WE WANT?" he said.

Cheers exploded. Chants.

"Sign 504! Sign 504! Unchanged! Sign 504 unchanged!"

I looked for Jeff Moyers, who was last on the roster of speakers. He was climbing onto the stage, guitar in hand. Standing in front of the crowd, black hair glistening, sunglasses cooler than cool, Jeff, who was low vision, started to sing. The crowd swayed in unison.

"Keep your eyes on the prize, hold on, hold on . . ." the crowd joined in, singing out loud, deaf people signing. People linked hands. The energy throbbed.

Taking a second or two to let the atmosphere sweep over me, I slowly moved my chair behind Jeff. It was almost time for me to say the words we'd agreed on.

The song ended. A silence crystallized, and grace rained over the quiet plaza.

Jeff stepped aside. I positioned my chair in front of the microphone. Softly, I motioned to Joe Quinn to move the microphone closer to me. Then, before anyone could move, I leaned up and yelled into the microphone: "Let's go and tell HEW the federal government cannot steal our civil rights!"

I turned and headed for the entrance to the Federal Building.

It was instant mayhem.

People surged behind me. Those who could walk went up the steps. Blind people pushed people in manual wheelchairs, the person in the wheelchair navigating. The people in electric chairs drove themselves up a ramp to the right of the steps.

Inside, people mobbed the atrium of the building. Someone pushed the button for the elevator. It was immediately crammed with people.

The elevator rose swiftly, past the first floor, to the fourth floor. Wheeling out, people gushed out of the other elevators into the hallway. The area teemed. People were pushing chairs, leaning on crutches, holding white canes.

Moving quickly but carefully, I wheeled down the hall and came to an office door marked "Regional Director, Federal Department of Health, Education, and Welfare." A deaf man opened the door for me, standing slightly to the side so I could squeeze my chair through the narrow doorway. I rolled up to the receptionist, who was sitting behind a white desk.

"We have a meeting with Joe Maldonado," I said to the woman. She looked alarmed.

Kitty came up behind me and said, "Wow!"

"Yeah, I never expected we'd get this many people." We were both thrilled.

Taking our names, the receptionist backed apprehensively away from us toward a door to her left. Behind us, more people spilled into the lobby, sitting in their wheelchairs, leaning against walls.

The receptionist came back.

"Mr. Maldonado will see you now. This way, please."

Kitty and I turned to follow her down the hallway. Immediately behind us were Mary Jane Owen, Jim, Steve McClelland, Joe Quinn, Mary Lou Breslin (another key organizer with us), and Ann Rosewater, a consultant from DC who worked with us on legal training.

I paused and turned back.

"Come with us," I said to a bunch of protesters in the reception area and gestured for them to follow. A considerable group trailed us into Maldonado's office.

Joe Maldonado was a smallish man with a head of graying curly hair. When we entered the room, he stood up and awkwardly motioned for us to sit, seeming not to process that many of us already were sitting.

"What can I do for you?" He was clearly shocked at the size of the crowd.

"We're here to ask about the status of the enabling regulations for Section 504 of the Rehabilitation Act." I spoke loudly.

Maldonado leaned back uneasily in his chair, with a guarded look. His light-colored suit was tight across his shoulders, a white polka dot tie resting on his chest. Behind me, more demonstrators packed themselves into the office.

The room hushed with attention.

"What is Section 504?" he asked.

I paused, surprised. What? Was he serious?

"Section 504 of Title V of the 1973 Rehabilitation Act prohibits discrimination against people with disabilities in institutions and programs receiving federal funding. HEW is responsible for finalizing the enabling regulations for it. Do you know anything at all about what is happening with these regulations in Washington?"

I hoped my voice was echoing down the hall to the rest of the protesters.

"I'm sorry, I don't know anything about Section 504 or about what is happening with these regulations," Maldonado said again, turning red.

Several worried wrinkles had appeared in his forehead.

"Can we please speak with the staff on your team who work on 504?" I asked.

Maldonado looked displeased. "I am telling you. We don't have any information for you."

"I understand," I said, "but we'd like to speak with your staff, please."

For a minute Maldonado looked like he was going to refuse. Then he walked out and came back a moment later with two HEW employees. I asked them about the regulations.

They looked utterly blank.

I explained again. Exasperation slipped into my voice. Joe Quinn stood behind me, interpreting in sign language.

The entire floor listened.

But it was true. Neither Maldonado nor his staff had any clue what I was talking about.

Hot fury consumed my body. This might just be a job to Maldonado, but his job affected people—every single person in his office and millions more. Did he not understand that?

With an icy calm, I bombarded Maldonado with question after question, asking why they were watering down the regulations, what changes were being proposed, why the department wasn't involving the community in the changes, when the regulations were coming out.

Maldonado looked like he was trying to disappear under his desk.

I refused to feel sorry for him. I leaned forward.

My heart pounded.

Now. Do it now, I thought.

I looked straight into Maldonado's eyes.

"504 is critical for our lives." I spoke vehemently, authoritatively. Behind me, I felt the crowd hold its breath.

"We're not leaving until we get assurances." The words came from some wellspring within me. A sense of absolute certainty spread throughout my body.

"You don't understand. You don't care," the crowd chanted behind me.

Maldonado looked at us. Perhaps he looked at us and saw a room full of people he could dismiss if he stared us down long enough. Then he got up and walked out of the office.

Kitty and I looked at each other. I leaned over to Kitty and whispered, "How did I do?" I always wanted to get Kitty's thoughts. Feeling my emotions as strongly as I did in these moments, it almost felt like an out-of-body experience, like I wasn't entirely sure of what had happened.

"You made mincemeat out of him." Kitty laughed.

I later learned that while we were with Maldonado, three female HEW employees had been walking around offering the protesters in the lobby cookies and punch they'd prepared for our meeting, like we were on some kind of field trip.

Evidently, they'd undercatered.

CHAPTER 6

OCCUPATION ARMY

AS SOON AS MALDONADO and the rest of the staff left for the night, Kitty and I gathered everyone in the main reception area of the office. It was a critical moment, and I was completely unprepared with any kind of speech. I spoke from my heart.

"We need you to stay with us in the building until the government signs the regulations for 504!" I told the crowd. "Please consider staying. We belong here."

For a long moment no one spoke.

For people with disabilities, a sleepover is not as simple as tossing some sandwiches and a toothbrush into a backpack. In addition to personal assistance, a fairly high number of us also require various types of daily medications and have things like catheters that need to be changed, or the need to get turned at night to avoid bedsores. Many people, of course, had come without a personal attendant, any kind of food, or even a toothbrush.

But slowly, one by one, hands went up and people started volunteering to stay. Some people rowdily shouted their support. Thankfully, a few personal attendants offered to stay.

In the end, seventy-five people committed to staying.

Exhilarated, Kitty and I went to Maldonado's office to re-group. Mary Lou, Mary Jane, Ann, and Jim came with us, as well as Pat Wright, a friend who helped me with personal assistance, and Joni Breves, another friend who'd driven Kitty to the rally. Joni was a real Brooklynite. She thought she was just driving Kitty to a protest, had no idea that the rally might turn into a sleepover, and ended up volunteering to stay.

Except for Joni and Ann, all of them had been on the committee we'd organized for 504. We'd had some quiet discussions about the possibility of a sit-in, but none of us had quite expected anything of this magnitude.

We looked at each other. What next? My mind raced.

"We need to figure out how we're going to feed everyone," Kitty said.

"I wonder what's happening with the other protests," Jim chimed in.

"We'd better come up with a plan for the press," I added.

We started planning.

Meanwhile, in the rest of the office, the protesters were introducing themselves to each other and spreading out to explore the space. The HEW offices were small, with large windows and a few couches and rugs scattered here and there. There was a good-sized conference room with an orange shag rug, which people immediately took over. Sitting around the table, chatting and laughing, they pulled candy bars and snacks out of their backpacks to share.

A sense of euphoria washed over the office. When you can't live independently, you don't get many chances to rebel.

From Maldonado's office we called the other protests and were delighted to discover that Denver and LA had also refused to leave the regional HEW offices, and DC, the national office, had also refused to leave. There were approximately fifty protesters in DC, seven in Denver, and twenty in LA. We were occupying four federal buildings.

The DC group was able to give us an update on Califano's reaction to the protests. When they refused to leave the office he rushed back from a trip just to meet with them. He must have been very flustered because he stood on top of an office coffee table to make an announcement. He told them that he was planning on signing the regulations—in May. He just needed a little longer to study them.

The minute we heard this, Kitty burst out: "He actually said he was going to *study* them?"

"Unbelievable," I said.

Pushing her blond hair off her face, Pat Wright was matter-of-fact: "He is still not getting this."

By that point the regulations had been being studied, commented on, and revised for three years. If Califano was still talking about studying them, without our input, then he clearly had no intention of working inclusively with us. If I had any doubts about what we were doing, they evaporated at that instant. I was weary beyond measure of people making decisions that affected our lives without consulting us.

The DC crew told us that Califano had left them in the HEW office but ordered that they be guarded. He'd given specific instruction that no food or medication was to be allowed into the office. Since that time, they said, they'd had only one glass of water and one donut each. As soon as they said this, I knew immediately what Califano was trying to do. He was going to try and starve them out.

We hung up with DC. Our attention shifted to figuring out how we were going to take care of the protesters in the building. We already had in place the committee structure that Kitty had created for the demonstration. We decided to turn that structure into a system that could support a big group of disabled people living in an office for an indefinite period of time. Right away we knew we'd need a committee to handle food, another to deal with medications, and one for press and PR. We also needed one to do outreach with our ally and partner organizations. More than ever, we needed the other civil rights groups to keep standing in solidarity with us. We also had to stay in touch with groups across disability: with the communities of the blind, the deaf, the cognitively disabled, and the parents of disabled kids. Although it was normal for us, the idea that our protest could represent all disabilities was going to be a change for the public to take on board. Our parents had organized according to their kid's type of disability. If they had a blind child, they allied with parents of blind kids, if their child had muscular dystrophy, the muscular dystrophy parents, and so forth. They'd seen disability as a particular problem of their child and a particular school's policy, not a wide-scale political issue. We who had come of age under the influence of Rosa Parks and Dr. Martin Luther King Jr., not to mention Gloria Steinem and the United Farm Workers, knew we were a band of underdogs fighting powerful institutions. If we didn't speak as one voice we'd never win.

Last, we added a committee for recreation. This many people in an enclosed space? We'd definitely need things to do.

To deal with food right away, we decided to call two of our allies—the Delancey Street Foundation, a rehabilitation program for drug addicts and ex-convicts, and the Salvation Army—to see if they might be willing to bring us meals for the next day, which they agreed to do.

With logistics taken care of for the moment, we started to discuss what would happen if there was a confrontation with the police. It was the '70s, we'd all been exposed to stories of violence associated with civil rights protests in the news, and we were in a group of adults in a small space. The HEW security guards, no doubt under instructions to maintain order, had locked the front doors in the face of protesters. Some men in suits and sunglasses, who looked like they could be FBI or Secret Service, had walked into the office after Maldonado left. Looking for someone to talk to amid the chaos of the protest, the men had connected with Joni. Perhaps because they thought she looked nondisabled and presumed she was in charge? We don't know, but she had, very intentionally, played on their fear of disability to get them to let more people into the building.

"Listen," she said, "unless you are going to help us with assisting people to go to the bathroom, and getting down on and up off the floor, we're going to need to get some more attendants into the building." They were so freaked out that they told Joni to give them a list of people to let in, which she'd taken advantage of by letting in as many of the locked-out protesters as possible. She also got people to call attendants and get them to come.

We decided to designate Joni as the official conduit of communication between us and HEW security, along with three other protesters. So that they could be easily identified, Jim suggested we make armbands for them. We called them the monitors.

At three in the morning we emerged from Maldonado's office. The protesters had found a way to sleep. Sprawled across the floor, they were lying hither and thither, head to toe, with a few of the personal attendants waking up to turn people. Looking for a place to bed down for the few hours left of the night, Jim and I ended up sleeping outside a freight elevator behind doors, Kitty and Mary Jane Owen slept in a closet off the conference room, and I'm not sure where Mary Lou, Pat, Joni, and Ann ended up.

The next morning I woke up with a start. Where was I? Then, feeling the hard floor beneath me, I remembered. I looked over at Jim; he was still sleeping. I checked my watch. Six in the morning. I'd only been asleep for about three hours, but that didn't surprise me. I've always been an early bird.

I poked Jim. I wanted to get up so we could find out what the press had said about us.

"An Occupation Army of Cripples Has Taken Over the San Francisco Federal Building" read one headline. Jim and I, along with Kitty, Pat, Mary Jane, and the rest of the leadership team, were gathered around Maldonado's desk. Newspapers were spread out in front of us, and the little television in Maldonado's office was on. Our sit-in was all over the Bay Area newspapers, television, and radio.

A television segment reported, "It all started this morning here at the Old Federal Building at 50 Fulton Street when an incident took place outside. Immediately after that demonstration this morning, the handicapped started invading the building."

We were being talked about as if we were a foreign army. The public was stunned. People weren't used to thinking of us as fighters—when they thought about us at all. And I don't say that in a bitter way, but in more of an honest way. We were a people who were generally invisible in the daily life of society. I mean, think about it. If you didn't see us in school, because we weren't allowed in; or at your place of employment, either because we couldn't physically access it or because we couldn't get hired; or on your form of public transportation, because buses and trains weren't accessible; or in restaurants or theaters, for the same reason—then where in your everyday life would you have seen us?

Well, I'll tell you where: probably on television. You might have seen Tiny Tim, who was "crippled," in *A Christmas Carol*, but more likely you would have associated us with telethons. At that time, Jerry Lewis was raising money on TV for muscular dystrophy; United Cerebral Palsy, for cerebral palsy; Easter Seals, for disability more broadly; and so on. No matter which telethon it was, though, a sick-looking child would have been trotted out with the express purpose of inspiring your sympathy, or rather, pity. These sick, pitiful images of disabled people contributed to the assumption that most folks had about us—that it was because of our medical condition that we weren't out and about in society. We were seen as helpless and childlike, as the kind of people for whom you felt pity and raised money to cure their disease. Not the kind of people who fought back.

It was time to share our side of the story. You can't just take over a federal building and not tell anyone why you did it.

We wrote a press release and announced that we'd be holding a press conference that afternoon in the HEW office. Maldonado and the HEW staff hadn't returned to their offices that morning—word was that they were working elsewhere in the building—so the PR committee had taken over the photocopy machine and fax in a little side room off the assistant director's office and designated it the press room. They sent our announcement to the media and then got on the phone to make sure reporters had received it. We were used to our issues and protests not receiving a great deal of attention, but now our activities thus far were getting some coverage and we wanted to keep up the momentum.

Downstairs, the security guards were allowing protesters to come and go, to get sleeping bags and clothes, go to medical appointments, and check in on their families.

Figuring out a method for keeping medications cold, Kitty taped a cardboard box over the air conditioner in Maldonado's office, created a makeshift refrigerator, and we went about the morning solving problems.

Around midafternoon, reporters started showing up for our press conference. We had organized for the meeting to take place in the large conference room. The protesters gathered. We'd prompted everyone to be prepared to sing protest songs when the media walked into the building, to link us to the civil rights movement. The leadership team assembled at the front of the room. With Joe interpreting, I opened the briefing as we'd planned. The first thing we did was educate them about terminology.

"Do not use the terms 'crippled,' or 'handicapped,' 'mute' or 'dumb,'" we told the reporters. "These are old terms and none of them are acceptable today. We are none of these things. We are people with disabilities." We went on to inform them about 504 and our position on the regulations. Listening, the reporters scribbled in their pads. Television cameras rolled.

What a pleasure it was to be able to teach them about discrimination and our civil rights.

"Quite frankly," I told one reporter from a national television station, "I think it's going to be very difficult for [HEW] to put a lot of pressure on us. When we asked them questions yesterday about 504 and we said to them, 'Have you ever read 504?' every single one of the people in that office said no. They should thank us for being here and welcome the opportunity that, finally, they're going to get educated about the law that they're supposed to be enforcing."

After the press conference, we learned about what had happened in Washington.

We were back in Maldonado's office.

"The DC protesters have left." Kitty was holding a press release in her hand from HEW.

"What? No!" I grabbed the press release from her hand and read it out loud to the group. There was a statement from Califano.

"The demonstration by the handicapped that ended this afternoon underscores the legitimate claim that this group has made on the American conscience. They have suffered discrimination that is wholly unjust. The 504 regulations that I will sign next month will, I believe, be a significant step toward remedying past

injustices suffered by the handicapped citizens in helping them
achieve the independence, dignity and fair treatment which is
theirs by right."[1]

"Bullshit," Pat said at my elbow.

We called DC to get the real story. It was just as we'd feared.
The protesters had had no access to food, medication, or phones,
and, one by one, people had left, starved out.

Califano had deliberately pushed them out, but because he
couldn't risk appearing antagonistic toward disabled people, he
had to simultaneously try to appear supportive of our cause. All
he had to do was bide his time, assuming people would lose interest if he reassured them that he was taking reasonable steps in
the face of our "irrational" actions.

"This is wrong."

The leadership team was clustered around us.

"He's deliberately misleading."

Right then and there, Mary Jane vowed to go on a hunger strike. In support, I committed to a hunger strike too. We
wanted to make the point that withholding food and supplies
from a group of peaceful demonstrators goes against the spirit
of democracy. A true democracy values the ability of citizens to
hold government accountable.

But now we were faced with a problem. We were in what was
only our first full day of occupation, and DC had already fizzled.
Califano was going to feel emboldened by how quickly he'd succeeded in pressuring us out. Certainly he would also know that
New York had shrunk down to ten people, Denver was hanging
on by a thread, and the Los Angeles protest was down to single
digits. He was going to be counting on our numbers dwindling.

We called a meeting of all the San Francisco protesters.

The Delancey Street Foundation and Salvation Army had
brought food, and people were just finishing dinner. Behind
closed doors we had prepped what we were going to say to the

protesters and I was charged with saying it. I'd become the designated lead communicator for the leadership team. I shared our analysis of Califano's strategy with the protesters.

"The DC protesters have left and we are losing momentum all over the country. Califano thinks that if he just waits we will fold. We need to prove him wrong. Even more than before, we need to stay in our position and hold strong. If we give up and lose this building, we will lose our only negotiating chip. It's become a waiting game." I paused. We couldn't ask people to stay indefinitely; that would be overwhelming. We could only ask people to commit to one day at a time.

"Can you stay one more night? Just one night will make a difference."

Again, one by one, the protesters started volunteering. Quietly, respectfully, everyone listened as each person in the room vowed to stay another night.

There were a hundred and ten people.

We'd grown by thirty-five people.

At the end, Jeff Moyer stood up and started playing "We Shall Overcome" on his guitar. Debbie Stanley, a blind protester with long straight hair and a beautiful voice, joined in. The next thing we knew, the crowd was singing.

"JUDY! JUDY! Wake up!"

Instantly awake, I opened my eyes. A monitor was standing in front of me, a serious look on his face.

"What's happening?" I looked at my watch. It was six in the morning.

Next to me, Jim sat up.

"I was just downstairs. The security guards aren't allowing anyone into the building. People can leave, but they can't come back in. Nobody can come back in. Judy, I think they've been ordered to completely shut down the building."

I looked at Jim and then back at the monitor. This was bad.

It was Good Friday.

If people wanted to go home to see their kids for the holiday they wouldn't be able to get back in. Not to mention the fact that this also meant no food could be brought in, no medications, no changes of clothes—nothing.

"People are going to start leaving," I said grimly.

Jim and I got up and went to assess the damage.

The hot water in the bathrooms had shut off. The office phone lines had been blocked for outgoing calls. Our only means of calling the outside world was two pay phones in the hallway.

Califano was tightening the noose.

At least we had access to televisions and radios in the office. We listened to the news.

"By now this demonstration here in San Francisco is clearly symbolic," said one reporter. "The group, which left the Washington, DC offices of HEW yesterday afternoon, were the only ones who really had direct access to Secretary Joseph Califano. Any demonstration here in San Francisco, well, can only be to show support. But it can't do anything tangible to get that anti-discrimination law signed right now."

We were being dismissed, just as Califano was hoping.

"Califano is trying to isolate us." I don't remember who said it first. I had, along with the rest of the leaders, immediately jumped into problem-solving mode. As usual, we were in Maldonado's office.

"We need to reach out to our partners and make it clear that we're bigger than our numbers in the building. What's he going to do next? He needs to know people are watching him," someone continued.

We called the Reverend Cecil Williams at Glide Memorial Church. Glide Memorial was a beacon of countercultural resistance in San Francisco and Reverend Williams was one of our staunchest supporters. We told him about the shutdown and asked for his help. On the spot, Cecil committed to organizing an ongoing vigil outside the building to call attention to our presence in the building. We then called Norman Leach from the Council of Churches, and he agreed to support the vigil.

We also added a paragraph to a press release we'd drafted the night before.

"Due to tightened security, people in support of our actions can no longer join us inside the Federal Building. Therefore, a vigil has begun on United Nations Plaza to give visible community support for our actions. All persons concerned with basic human rights are urged to join the vigil, which will offer support for those who are in the building." The PR team faxed the statement to the press.

But the day was just beginning.

"HEW is not studying the regulations anymore." Ann Rosewater had news from her contacts on the Hill in DC. The rest of us gathered around to listen.

"Califano is working on a major redirection," she continued. "They have a list of issues. They're looking at potentially excluding a whole generation of buildings from compliance, leaving alcoholics and drug addicts out of the regulations, and creating some sort of university consortia that allows universities to avoid becoming accessible. It would essentially require disabled students to attend classes at only certain universities."

Silence.

Finally, Pat spoke.

"It is still separate but equal in a new form."

Kitty said what we were all thinking. "They're not taking us seriously at all."

———

NOT LONG AFTER, we found out that Denver and New York City had folded. They'd had no personal assistance or accessible bathrooms.

Now Califano was going to be even more sure that we were on the verge of falling apart.

Sitting in Maldonado's office, looking at the somber faces of Kitty, Pat, Mary Jane, Joni, Jim, and Mary Lou, I fought a feeling of hopelessness.

All of a sudden, a member of the outreach committee burst in.

"Governor Brown has endorsed us! He's written a letter to President Carter urging him to sign the regulations! We're getting endorsements from all kinds of labor unions, churches, and civil rights groups! The United Farm Workers have sent a telegram of support—Cesar Chavez signed it himself!"

For a minute, we just stared at her, unable to process what she was saying.

Then we cheered.

People were paying attention. California's governor, Jerry Brown, was paying attention. They were listening. They supported us.

We just had to hold on and figure out how to turn up the volume on Califano. We talked for a long time. That was when Pat Wright started to emerge as a brilliant strategist. Her ability to see the chess board four moves ahead would prove pivotal in the years to come.

We decided we should try and go over Califano's head. We would try and get to President Carter.

The LA protesters were still hanging in there, with something like thirty-five protesters. We called to tell them what we were thinking. If we were going to reach President Carter, we had to coordinate with them. Luckily, they were fully supportive of the idea.

We managed to get Carter's director of scheduling on the phone. We asked for a meeting with the President and she promised to get back to us. But something in the way she said it made me think, "I'm not holding my breath."

The protesters filed into the conference room. People were starting to look a little unwashed and ragged. Everything depended on our ability to convince them to stay. We were sure that the only way to maintain the group was to create an overwhelming sense of unity—and the only way to do that was to be totally inclusive and completely open. We waited until every single person had arrived and the sign language interpreters were ready to start translating.

When it was quiet, I began to speak.

"The situation is this: President Carter knows where we stand. The White House is supposed to be calling us. The call has not come through yet.

"The shutdown is serious, but we are gaining momentum. In the last few hours, we've been getting national attention. An endorsement from Governor Brown has just come in.

"We cannot leave. LA is the only other sit-in still going, and they're holding on with just thirty-five people. We're the biggest.

"We are asking you if you can you stay? Can you? Every day will make a difference."

Then, as before, people committed to staying. Some spoke emotionally about their belief in what we were doing. Others offered ideas to help.

"I can call the Black Panthers." It was Brad Lomax, a young protester with multiple sclerosis who used a wheelchair and favored suits with wide lapels. Brad was a member of the Black Panthers, whom we'd partnered with at various times.

Other protesters asked questions about 504 and our political strategy. People were still on a steep learning curve. People had been internalizing the idea that our barriers were our individual problem for so long it was hard to shift. People had to get out of the habit of thinking "I can't get up the steps because I can't walk" and get used to thinking "I can't get up the steps because they're not accessible." Ann offered to do trainings on 504 and policy.

Members of the recreation committee talked about organizing events for Easter and Passover.

The energy in the room was palpable. We kept the meeting going until every last protester had had their say.

In the end, when all one hundred twenty-five protesters had committed to staying, I felt better, although I felt very responsible. Even though about ten of us were on a hunger strike, I didn't know how the hell we were going to feed everybody else.

The shutdown had cut us off almost entirely from the outside world. The committees immediately got to work, trying to solve the problems of getting food and medications into the building, and handling the upcoming holiday weekend.

The leadership team reconvened in Maldonado's office. I had to stop and get some water. It was the third day of our hunger strike and all I'd had was water and an occasional juice. I wasn't tired at all, though. I was running on adrenaline and I've always had a high level of energy.

We talked about how to break through the isolation Califano had imposed on us. How could we stay in regular touch with our allies and the press? The stream of articles and public declarations we'd been getting were putting pressure on HEW and the administration. We had to keep the articles coming. If we didn't we would fade into irrelevance. But how?

Then it occurred to us. We had a secret weapon.

Sign language.

We decided to give our announcements and messages to the deaf protesters, who took them to the windows looking out on the plaza, where our supporters were holding the vigil. When they got the attention of the deaf protesters and sign language interpreters outside, they signed our messages through the window. The deaf protesters and sign language interpreters then relayed the messages to the right people.

It was beautiful.

Our second secret weapon came from a totally unexpected direction: HEW itself.

Very early on, we had determined that we would act with the utmost respect and friendliness toward the HEW staff and security guards in the building. The friendly policy was slowly having an effect. Our behavior, along with the fairness of our cause, was gradually winning the sympathies of the HEW employees. That day, a hundred employees signed a petition in support of us and sent it to Califano. The HEW regional assistant director, Bruce Lee, whose father was blind, had been applying pressure to Maldonado to push Califano to sign; that Friday he also started using a warning system with us, turning his lapel pin upside down to tell us when security guards were coming. All of these things helped undermine Califano's position.

WE WERE IN MALDONADO'S office later that afternoon when one of the protesters came quickly rolling in.

"The Black Panthers are forcing their way into the building!"

Zooming out of the office, we rolled down the hallway just as the fourth-floor elevator doors slid open. I couldn't quite process what I was seeing. Six tall African American men wearing slouchy hats, sweater vests, and black leather jackets walked off the elevator carrying plastic tubs.

"We told the security guards we would stop at nothing to bring the media's attention on HEW if they didn't let us in and you guys got starved out." One of them said to me, "We've got dinner and snacks here." The Black Panthers, called by Brad Lomax, had pushed their way into the building with fried chicken and vegetables, walnuts, and almonds. They had brought food for all 125 of us. We all gathered around, amazed, talking and laughing, clapping and cheering. It was like an enormous gust of wind had just filled our sail and pushed us forward.

The Black Panthers brought us food every night for the rest of the protest.

In the evening news, the press came out.

One TV news show reported, "They're tired. They're grubby. They're uncomfortable. But their spirits are soaring. The sit-in in the San Francisco HEW headquarters is now in its third day. A hundred and twenty-five disabled and handicapped are pledging they'll continue the sit-in through tomorrow night, if not longer. The squeeze is on, though. Hot water has been turned off on the fourth floor, where the occupation army of cripples has taken over."

That night, a group of the protesters and I lit a candle and held a Shabbat dinner in the freight elevator.

"JUDY! KITTY!" I was in Maldonado's office drinking a cup of water with Kitty and a few others a little later, enjoying the brief sense of calm the Panthers' visit had brought, when Joni came rushing into the room.

"The security guards say that we have to get everyone out of the building because there's a bomb."

Kitty and I looked at her.

"Hmmm. What did they say exactly?" I asked.

"It was three or four of those security guards that wear the big black boots. They came and found me and said, 'You have to get everyone out of the building. There's a bomb.' They had a bomb-sniffing German Shepherd with them. They looked very threatening."

Kitty and I looked at each other. She shrugged a little, and I knew what she was thinking. It was way too coincidental.

"I don't care," I said. "I'm going to bed. Tell them to wake me up when it goes off."

"Yup, me too," Kitty said.

We had to tell the protesters about the warning, just in case anybody wanted to leave. We called an emergency meeting and told them what the security guards had said and what we'd decided, offering for people to leave if they were uncomfortable. Nobody left.

When I woke up the next morning, I looked at my watch. Five a.m. The building was still standing. No bomb. I lay there for a few minutes and thought about the day. It was Saturday, April 9, our fourth day in the building. It was also the seventh day of Passover, which I normally celebrated but hadn't had any time to think about. Now, the symbolism hit me. The deliverance of the Israelites from slavery. Freedom. Lying there on the floor, in the dark of early morning, I smiled to myself. My body was sore from sleeping on the floor and I hadn't eaten for days, but I felt good.

I poked Jim. "Let's get up. I want to wash my hair." Cold water or not, I hate dirty hair.

Dressed and with nice fresh clean hair, I sat for a minute talking with Jim while people slowly woke up around us. Jim drank a cup of coffee and I had some water. I've never been a coffee drinker, never been a caffeine drinker, actually. At that moment, a monitor found us.

"Judy, the last two pay phones are jammed. No one can make any calls."

We were totally cut off from making any outgoing calls.

That afternoon Carter's secretary of scheduling got a message through to us.

"The president is aware of the situation in Los Angeles and San Francisco," she said. "He gives you his assurance that he will become personally involved in the issue of 504 and the issue of the regulations."

We issued a response and gave it to our signers at the window to communicate: "We are encouraged by the contact made with the White House. However, the statement is not adequate, for Carter failed to address the primary reason for this sit-in. That is, the regulations of January 21 must be signed. The proposed changes from Califano are nonnegotiable. Changes Califano is reviewing are nonacceptable and nonnegotiable."

The LA protesters had gotten the same message from Carter's director of scheduling, but unable to reach us and unsure what to do, they'd finally just decided to take her at her word. They'd left the building.

We were the last city standing.

That night, the news programs called us the "largest and longest protest ever organized by disabled people in this area" but claimed that the problem was still "the same as it was on Tuesday: trying to get the attention of the people in Washington."

The next morning was both Easter and the last day of Passover. I could see through the windows that it was going to be a beautiful sunny day.

That morning I decided to break my hunger strike. I needed all my strength and energy to think and strategize.

People were feeling festive. The recreation committee organized an Easter service and egg hunt for the protesters' children inside the building, who were allowed in by security guards willing to look the other way. Out in front of the building, our supporters kept up the vigil with a special Easter service.

Despite the holiday, the leadership team didn't pause. While the kids looked for Easter eggs and the rally was in full force outside, we were in Maldonado's office, talking on the telephone to HEW's general counsel, Peter LiBossi. Peter had taken to calling us to check in, mainly to determine whether there was a way to get us to vacate the building. Talking with Peter was a game of chicken. His goal was to try and persuade us to trust HEW and their process so we would leave, and our goal was to ferret out from him as much information as possible. He had to share some information with us to try and appear as if he was on our side—but not too much information, and nothing that would harden our resolve to stay. That day he was erring on the side of oversharing, as he talked a bit too freely about some of the changes under discussion at HEW that would take the regulations far beyond where we wanted them.

Along with Pat Wright and Kitty, I was sitting and listening to Peter when California congressman George Miller suddenly walked in, completely unannounced. George Miller was around our age—he was just thirty-two. Figuring out right away that we were on the phone with someone in DC, Miller quietly walked over to another phone and picked up the receiver.

Silently he listened in as Peter talked about the changes HEW was considering.

"Peter," he interrupted, "this is Congressman George Miller."

Abruptly Peter stopped talking.

I don't remember what was said after that exactly, but Peter basically hung up very quickly.

The congressman put the phone down and turned to all of us in the room, a serious look on his face.

"Stay," he said. "Stay in this building and don't leave until you've won."

The next day Congressman Miller called to tell us that he and California congressman Phil Burton had agreed to hold a congressional hearing in the building. On Friday, at the end of the week.

"Hooray!" we cheered, elated. It was a huge victory. A congressional hearing is a way for Congress to investigate, through the testimony of the public and experts, what's going with an issue. The fact that the representatives were not only planning on holding a congressional hearing but were planning on holding it *in the building*, meant that we had succeeded in elevating our issues to the point where Congress was getting involved with real sincerity.

CHAPTER 7

SOLDIERS IN COMBAT

AVRIL HARRIS, one of the few attendants still in the building on the Monday morning after Easter, was developing a schedule. She'd wake Kitty up with a cup of coffee, then look for me to see if I needed anything. That morning she'd helped me wash my hair again and then Jim and I went to look for Pat, Mary Jane, Kitty, Ann, and Joni. Mary Lou had gotten sick over the weekend and had had to go home.

We found Mary Jane with Jeff Moyer and Debbie Stanley in the lobby. The two had decided to kick off the new week by serenading the HEW employees into the building as they arrived for work. Alongside them a small group of protesters were handing out daffodils.

We'd been in the building almost a week and we were settling into a kind of routine. In the mornings, the various committees would meet. The food committee planned meals and the medications committee compiled a list of needs. The Buttercup Restaurant, Brick Hut Lesbian Cooperative in Berkeley, and Glide Memorial were donating food, in addition to the hot meals from the Black Panthers. Local pharmacists were helping with medications and other items. Sometime in the late afternoon or early evening we would hold a buildingwide meeting to share what we knew of events happening outside the building and our current thinking on strategy. As had become our practice, the leadership team would hash through an approach, which Kitty and I would then present to the larger group. We continued to maintain our policy of not starting the meetings until every single protester had arrived and the sign language interpreters were ready to start, and we insisted that the meetings not end until every last protester had had the chance to speak. This sometimes meant that our meetings didn't end until three in the morning, partly because some of us struggled with forming words as a result of our disability and partly because we were dealing with issues we took very seriously.

The most remarkable thing about our buildingwide meetings wasn't their length, however, but the culture of listening that developed. No matter how long it took for someone to talk, we listened. Every one of the now one hundred and fifty protesters would listen in a perfect and beautiful silence. When Hale Zukas pointed out one letter at a time on his board with the makeshift pointer stick attached to his head, the room swelled with a gracious quiet. We treasured the ability to create our own space, where our communication needs, and their slower pacing, were respected.

To be clear, "discomfort and anxiety was the order of our day-to-day existence," as one demonstrator would later say. Many of us were taking the risk of depending on strangers for personal assistance. One protester, Bill Blanchard, would remember "spending the first couple of nights sleeping in my chair because it meant less transferring and less having to ask strangers for assistance." People were going without things like backup catheters, ventilators, and other equipment that, if they were to fail, could mean life or death for us. [1]

But despite the discomfort, people began to have fun. They raced their wheelchairs in the halls, organized games, played the guitar and sang songs. There was almost no privacy. Everyone was getting dressed and taking care of whatever they needed to do in the middle of everything, and they were bonding. They sat in small circles for hours, talking and talking. Friendships formed. A young disabled woman fell in love with an attendant and talked about how this made her feel beautiful for the first time in her life. Ed's friend Werner Erhard, the founder of est, a program he developed to help people transform their mind-set, showed up and volunteered to hold workshops for the protesters. Civil rights leaders such as the high-profile Georgia state senator Julian Bond visited us. The Black Panthers came and stayed to hang out. Two well-known psychologists offered workshops on sex and disability.

It was, after all, the '70s.

It was sex, drugs, and rock and roll. Long hair, bell bottoms, and self-expression. Jefferson Airplane, Queen, and the Eagles.

For those of us who'd grown up with a disability, the sit-in may have felt more like camp than anything else. Camp was the one other time in our lives when we'd lived in a world that worked for us and our needs. Where we didn't have to feel inferior for being slow or different. For being a burden. Where we could be ourselves without apology. In the building, just as at camp, we could easily visit each other and spend time together without having to rely on a family member, or a friend, or unreliable public transportation. The inaccessibility of the outside world, which so often left us isolated, felt very far away.

At the same time, the reporters following our story were becoming captivated by us. Evan White, a reporter with San Francisco's *ABC News*, on Channel 7, borrowed a wheelchair and used it all day in downtown San Francisco, then reported on the experience.

New endorsements were coming in from all directions. Protesters in DC and Madison, Wisconsin, held vigils in our honor.

We were becoming a part of something bigger than ourselves. As CeCe Weeks, a young blond quadriplegic protester, said to television reporters, "It's the first really militant thing that disabled people have ever done. We feel like we're building a real social movement."

I've never experienced another social movement in the same way, but I wonder if the bonding that we felt, becoming as intimate as soldiers in combat, is how all social movements feel from the inside.

FRIDAY, APRIL 15, was the eleventh day of the sit-in and the day of the congressional hearing. Congressman Miller and Congressman Burton walked into the building and declared room 406 a satellite office of Congress. I remember it as a small room chockfull of people. There were people in wheelchairs, mentally disabled people, parents, deaf people signing, and blind people with white canes, along with a sprinkling of reporters and media. Eight hundred additional protesters gathered outside our building for a rally. Senator Alan Cranston, the Democratic whip, sent our group a telegram of support.

Congressman Burton opened the proceedings by stating that the intention of the hearing was to understand the nature of the conflict. Joe Quinn stood next to him, translating in sign language. I spoke first.

"You have given us respectability," I said, thanking the congressmen. "We will not compromise any further.

"We will not be leaving this building until the regulations are signed as we want. This is a civil rights movement." I paused, then continued, "You are helping us start a civil rights movement."

Gene Eidenberg, the HEW representative from Washington, then read a statement on behalf of Secretary Califano and the undersecretary. The statement essentially repeated what we all already knew, that the regulations were under review.

The congressmen asked Eidenberg why signing the regulations was being delayed.

Eidenberg demurred, quoting issues of studies and reviews. Clearly, he'd been given his marching orders by the higher-ups at HEW. The fact that Califano even sent a somewhat lower-level bureaucrat to a congressional hearing spoke volumes about his attitude toward us.

The congressmen probed Eidenberg's responses. What studies? For what purpose, exactly?

Eidenberg, growing obviously uncomfortable under their scrutiny, remained opaque. Awkwardly, he tried to explain HEW's position. Rambling, he mentioned the words "separate but equal" and in the same sentence dropped the news that the number of issues under review had reached a total of twenty-six.

The instant I heard this phrase something exploded inside me.

Still "separate but equal"? HEW was *still* considering a "separate-but-equal" approach? After all the support we'd gotten from the civil rights groups? Had they never heard of *Brown v. Board of Education*? In no other area of civil rights would the concept of "separate but equal" be tolerated, much less discussed with such insistence.

My insides churned with anger and frustration.

While I was desperately trying to maintain my composure in the front of the room, Kitty slipped out the back. The minute Eidenberg had uttered the words "separate but equal," she turned her chair around and rolled out the door. In front of the building, as the congressional hearing continued indoors, Kitty told the assembled crowd outdoors what Eidenberg had said about "separate but equal."

The eight hundred protesters dissolved in an uproar so loud we could hear it inside.

It was my turn to respond to the statement Eidenberg had read.

I didn't look at my notes.

Taking a deep breath, I looked directly at Eidenberg.

"Whether there was a Section 504," I said, my voice breaking, "there was a *Brown v. Board of Education*." My voice broke again. I looked down, swallowed my tears, and looked back up at Eidenberg.

"The . . ." I stopped, suddenly overwhelmed by the weight and exhaustion of the days, the weeks, the years of pushing. Of having to fight, just for an equal chance to live.

I took another deep breath.

"The harassment. The lack of equity that has been provided for disabled individuals, and that even now is being discussed by the administration, is so intolerable that I can't quite put it into words." I could not keep my voice from trembling. With every word, I felt a memory weighing. Of being in my living room by myself, staring out the window, while all my friends were in school. At Brooklyn College, crying as my father carried me onto the stage. Knocking on doors in my dorm, looking for help to go to the bathroom. The flight attendants trying to throw me off the plane, all the passengers' eyes on me.

"I *can* tell you," I said, a force rising in me, "that every time you raise issues of 'separate but equal,' the outrage of disabled individuals across this country is going to continue, is going to be ignited. And there will be more takeovers of buildings until, finally, *maybe*, you'll begin to understand our position.

"We will no longer allow the government to oppress disabled individuals. We want the law enforced! We want no more segregation! We will accept no more discussions of segregation and . . ."

I paused. Eidenberg was nodding sympathetically at me. The look on his face was unbearable.

"And, I would appreciate it if you would stop nodding your head in agreement when I don't think you have any idea what we are talking about!" I put my head in my hands and choked back my tears. The room burst in applause.

The next hour of testimony was a blur. So many people spoke.

"What Califano forgets is that while they sit around and intellectualize, what they don't seem to understand is that our lives are not changed," said Debbie Kaplan of the Disabilities Rights Center in DC.

Ed Roberts said, "For one of the largest minorities in the country, I have never seen a better blueprint for segregation."

Denise Darensbourg, who was developmentally disabled, stated, "I might seem second class to them, but I'm a person like everyone else. I don't think it's fair to be put down. I went to a special school for the mentally retarded. I didn't learn the things I should have. The attitude was that I couldn't learn anyway, so why bother? I need help with some things, but not with all."

In the midst of it all, Eidenberg seemed unable to decide his position. One minute he appeared pitying, the next unreadable, then frustrated.

One by one, speaker after speaker got up, blind, deaf, physically disabled, former addicts, parents of disabled, sharing thoughts, feelings, pain, isolation, anger, heartbreak, telling of years spent trying to get a job, an education, trying to count, trying to matter.

Suddenly, Eidenberg abruptly stood up from the table, turned, and ran out the door.

I looked at the congressmen. Everyone was looking at each other, confused. What had just happened? Did Eidenberg really just run out of the room?

Down the hallway, a door slammed.

Congressman Burton jumped up. Red in the face, he turned around and dashed out the door after Eidenberg.

"Get out of there! Come out of there right now! Get out of there!" We heard him yell, kicking the door.

Utter silence.

"Come out here! Get out here right now!" Congressman Burton was livid.

Finally, we heard a door open.

Eidenberg walked back into the room, shadowed by Congressman Burton. He looked down, clearly avoiding our eyes. Ashamed.

Fists clenched, Congressman Burton walked behind him, escorting him back to his chair. He stood behind him and waited until Eidenberg had sat down again and then forced him to face us.

The hearing continued. It was five hours of testimony.

Congressman Burton wrapped up. "I don't believe there is a person in this room who is not standing ten feet taller because of today," he said, tears in his eyes.

After the hearing, we were sure we would hear something from Califano.

We heard nothing.

WE LEADERS MET behind closed doors, frustrated.

What did we have to do to make it impossible for Califano to ignore us?

We had to find a way to raise the stakes even more.

"What if we sent a delegation to DC?" I asked.

If a group of protesters went to Washington we could have face-to-face meetings with the congressmen and -women who had sponsored 504, and we could try to get to Califano and President Carter. I knew from my experience on Capitol Hill that face-to-face meetings were always better. Right now, our distance was allowing DC to dismiss us and marginalize us as West Coast radicals. The *Washington Post*'s coverage of the sit-in had been very limited. If we went to Washington with the moral authority of the sit-in behind us, people would be forced to take us seriously. It could be a bold move. But it also came with a lot of risk. If we failed, we could get blocked from reentering the San Francisco Federal Building and lose our base in the building, our only bargaining chip.

At the same time, we were very aware of the fact that at any moment we could become old news in San Francisco. The protesters were riding high on excitement and adrenaline, but what if we continued to be ignored? Or worse, ridiculed? The protesters' mood could turn on a dime.

We had to act.

It was now or never.

THE DAY AFTER the hearing we put the decision to the protesters. There was no way we could send a delegation to DC without the full agreement and support of all one hundred fifty protesters. If people felt they were getting left behind because they were less important than the delegates, they could fall into conflict and we'd risk losing the building.

As always, we waited for all the protesters to arrive, and then waited until the sign language interpreters were ready to start signing.

I was nervous.

There were many major decisions to be made.

First, we had to agree on the basic idea of sending a delegation, which was already a big decision for a large group of people to make.

Once we made that decision, we would have to agree on the *timing* of the delegation. We had floated the idea of sending a delegation by the DC protesters, and they had asked us to delay our trip to give them time to organize before we came. We thought that the DC protesters felt unnecessarily bad about how their sit-in had folded and might be worried that it looked like we were coming to their rescue. But we couldn't wait; our sit-in could dissolve at any moment. We had to share the DC group's request with our group, though, so they could decide together whether or not they wanted to honor it. So that was the second decision.

Third, we had to vote on the makeup of the delegation: Who would go to DC? And what size group made sense?

It would have been a lot for any group of a hundred fifty people to process, but throw in people's disabilities, the methodical pace of our communication, and the varying cognitive abilities represented in the room, and we were facing a challenging meeting.

Sitting in front of all the protesters, I paused. As a woman, I knew I walked a fine line between being seen as "strong" and being seen as "unlikable." I was aware that if we decided to go against the wishes of our colleagues in DC they might get upset and blame me. But I had to be honest.

Speaking as deliberately and clearly as I could, I talked about the reasoning behind the potential delegation and shared the request of the DC protesters.

"We have been the strongest and lasted the longest. Washington has fizzled twice. We have to watch out for our own position. One or two days might make us fizzle. This is a day-to-day, if not hour-to-hour, situation."

I stopped and waited. What else could I say? It was simply the truth.

Later, one of the protesters recalled later that I came across as "calmly unstoppable" and asked herself, "Who wouldn't follow this woman?"

But this is not how it felt on the inside. On the inside, waiting to hear the protesters' perspective, I was not at all sure of where we were going. All I knew was that we would have no power at all if we weren't united.

The group talked and talked and talked. Until, beautifully, amazingly, everyone agreed. We would send a delegation as soon as possible.

A committee of eight was appointed to select the group that would go to DC and was charged with the responsibility of ensuring that the delegation be representative of disability and race. Evan White, the *ABC News* reporter, committed to joining the delegation. CeCe Weeks and Ray Uzeta, who worked at CIL, were designated the directors of the San Francisco sit-in while the leadership team was in DC.

Now we just had to raise the money for the trip.

The next day was Sunday, April 17. It had been a week since Easter and Passover. That morning, the Reverend Cecil Williams's sermon at Glide Memorial Church was about the sit-in. In attendance was a man by the name of Willy Dicks. Dicks was a member of the International Association of Machinists, one of the oldest labor unions in America and famous for fighting inequality. Willy came straight from the sermon to our building, a check for $1,000 in his hand.

Willy told us that Reverend Williams had asked, in his sermon, "If those people can sit there, what's the matter with the rest of you?" So Willy had come to ask us what he could do to help. It was another one of those synchronicities that would change everything. Over the next two days, Willy got the Machinists on board with our cause and raised the money to pay for our thirty-four-person delegation's trip to DC.

That same Sunday San Francisco's mayor, George Moscone, showed up at the building with the medical director of San Francisco General Hospital and a host of other health officials in tow. Mayor Moscone, who at the time was pushing to integrate women and racial minorities into the city commissions, was famous for protecting the interests of people with less power. He brought soap, towels, cream for wheelchair sores, and flexible hoses with shower heads to attach to the bathroom faucets so people could bathe. He asked people to line up so that they could have any uncared-for medical needs attended to by the medical officials.

Maldonado pushed back on the mayor's help, allowing him to attach just one shower head. "We're not running a hotel," he said. Obviously he was still hoping we'd become so uncomfortable that we'd leave.

Mayor Moscone was fuming. He vowed to call President Carter, and he did, and he got permission to attach all four showers.

It was an unbelievable day.

Just six months later, the gay rights activist Harvey Milk would be elected San Francisco's first openly gay city supervisor, with Mayor Moscone's support. Tragically, Moscone would end up paying for this with his life when both he and Milk were assassinated by a conservative former supervisor, Dan White.

But that day, Mayor Moscone played a pivotal role in what was to come.

CHAPTER 8

THE WHITE HOUSE

OUR PLANE ARRIVED at Dulles International Airport late, around nine-thirty at night.[1]

"Welcome to Washington!" said Willy Dicks, standing in the cabin of our plane. He was a sight for our tired eyes. We were sweaty and dirty and, because of our lengthy late-night meetings, had had very little sleep for days. Willy, wearing a hip three-piece suit and Afro, was with an older white-haired man dressed in conservative attire—the two making a somewhat odd couple. The white-haired man turned out to be George Robinson—called Robin—the president of International Association of Machinists District 141 in Chicago.

We were now two weeks into the sit-in, and three days had passed since we'd voted to send a delegation to Washington. Since showing up at the building on Sunday, Willy had mobilized his fellow Machinists around the country. They, along with Werner Erhard, who had made a donation, had raised the money for our flights, facilitated our travel arrangements, set up a temporary office for us in their DC headquarters, and were even hosting a reception to welcome us to Washington. They had boarded the plane to help those of us in wheelchairs get off. There were thirty-four people in our delegation, many of whom were wheelchair users, and we didn't have enough personal attendants for everyone. Willy and Robin's help with personal assistance was a lifesaver.

Rolling into the airport, we found the leaders of the DC protesters waiting for us—Frank Bowe and Eunice Fiorito and a few others. Immediately they started trying to explain.

"We were starved out of HEW," Eunice said. "The organizing climate in the East is not the same as the West. Our people haven't come out the way we think they should. We haven't gotten any press. The kids of Gallaudet [a university for deaf students in DC] marched for two days in the rain and no cameras ever came."

We all spoke at once, saying things like "Eunice, what happened to you motivated us to stay. We were outraged by how you were treated."

"Eunice, you don't have to apologize," Hale Zukas told her.

I wanted her, all of them, to understand how connected we felt to their experience. In no way was what happened their fault. Eunice was right about the difference between the East and West Coasts. It *was* harder to organize people with disabilities on the East Coast. Transportation was a big problem. The DC Metro wasn't accessible and the city was spread out. Motorized wheelchairs were less common and there was less access to and support for attendant services. Nothing like the Center for Independent Living existed, and overall there were fewer people living independently in the community, the way we did in the Bay Area. All of which made it much harder for people with disabilities to move around on their own and, as a result, harder for us to organize them.

We exited the airport. "You're gonna have to ride in a truck," Willy had told us when he boarded the plane. "It's going to be uncomfortable, but you're used to that. I'm going to ride back there with you." They'd rented a giant Ryder moving truck, which at the time was the cheapest and most accessible way to transport thirty-four disabled people around DC. Together, we rolled out to the truck the Machinists had rented.

The Machinists, along with Ralph Abascal, an attorney, Phil Neumark, the deputy director of the California Department of Rehabilitation, and Olin Fortney, one of the deaf protesters, loaded us onto the lift and into the back of the truck. The truck had no windows and was pitch black. There were no tie-downs and no warnings for turns. Every time we turned a corner we got tossed around.

"Whoa!" we shouted.

We decided to go straight to Califano's house.

Califano lived in a well-to-do DC neighborhood, on a cul-de-sac called Springland Lane. It turned out to be directly across the street from Kitty's great-aunt and -uncle, and down the street from their son, Kitty's cousin, and his wife and kids. This crazy coincidence would later mortify Kitty, in a bunch of funny ways.

Unloading in the dark, we got everyone out of the truck, made a circle in front of Califano's house, and lit candles.

The East Coast protesters had been against the idea of going to Califano's home: it broke certain conventions for how people practiced civil protest. But we had voted to go anyway. I was too angry to worry about protocol. Califano's power rested in his ability to ignore us. The only way we were going to change anything was if we became impossible to ignore. My feeling is that when you're addressing power you have to do whatever you can to get their attention, as long as it isn't violent.

We sat in front of Califano's large brick colonial house all night, softly singing freedom songs and hymns. At dawn, a pastor from a local church, the Reverend Ken Longfield, held an early-morning prayer service.

As the sky streaked pink and yellow, Kitty's cousin Jimmy, who had been a general in the army, jogged past. He did a double take.

"Kitty!" he said, totally surprised. "How lovely. You're having a prayer service." Quietly, he took a place in our circle. Blushing, Kitty gave him a hug and did not enlighten him as to why we were there.

We saw nothing of Califano nor of anyone in his house.

We piled back into the truck to go to Reverend Longfield's church, Luther Place Memorial, where the Machinists had organized for us to stay. They'd gotten permission to tear down walls in the bathroom and put in ramps to make the space accessible. From Califano's house it was about a forty-five-minute drive to Luther Place Memorial in downtown DC.

At the church we all took a few minutes to catch our breath. We needed some breakfast and a lot of people needed coffee. Even I had a few sips of coffee, which I only drank when I was really tired. The second week we'd been in the Federal Building, some of the building employees had taken to bringing the garbage up the freight elevator at three in the morning and clanging it around, clearly instructed by someone to make as much noise as possible. I was still operating with very little sleep, but I didn't feel bad. I was in high gear.

We gathered around a table in the back of the church to discuss tactics.

If our primary goal was to make it impossible for Califano to continue ignoring us, there were a few key things we needed to do. We'd lined up meetings with the two original sponsors of the 504 legislation, Senator Harrison Williams, whom I'd worked for as a legislative assistant, and Senator Alan Cranston, the Democratic whip. We wanted both of them to publicly state that they were in agreement with the 504 regulations as originally drafted and that they did not agree with any of HEW's changes.

In addition to gaining congressional support, we had to reach as high as we possibly could in the executive branch: the White

House. We had to try and get a meeting with President Carter or one of his top policy people.

Finally, we had to keep the pressure on Califano turned up high, which meant more candlelight vigils and demonstrations in front of his home. With press coverage.

We packed ourselves in to the truck for our first two meetings and drove to Capitol Hill.

A tall man with a bald head and a sharp intelligence, Senator Alan Cranston was a World War II veteran and a former journalist. He was also a very political, powerful liberal crusader. If we could persuade him to issue a statement, it would have a tremendous impact on Califano and Carter.

Cranston assured us that he found our actions reasonable.

"I do think the people responsible for the laws should hear the people affected," he said. But then he pushed back hard. He was a tough man, known in Washington as a dealmaker, and he didn't mince words.

"I'm not an administration spokesman," he said.

We had to convince him to see things from our perspective before he would be willing to be more helpful. He wanted to know what he was supposed to do for us.

"We've sought meetings with President Carter and Secretary Califano. We were unsuccessful," I told him, feeling slightly intimidated to be confronting him face-to-face.

"You are prejudging their changes. The Carter administration changes may make [the regulations] more effective."

I steeled myself. Senator Cranston was going to need to hear a very clear, very rational, very intelligent argument.

The senator had a list of the changes proposed by HEW. Although the list was lengthening on a daily basis, it boiled down to ten main points, every single one of which watered down the regulations. One of them referred to the creation of the

"separate-but-equal" consortium of universities; another allowed delay and lack of compliance for new construction; yet
another gave existing buildings a loophole for renovations. The
controversial question of whether or not drug addicts and alcoholics would be included in the definition of people with
disabilities was still on the table. Every point was nonnegotiable for us.

One by one, Cranston went over the issues. One by one, a
different person in the delegation responded to him, answering
his objections very thoroughly, very persuasively.

Still, Cranston challenged us.

I pushed back.

"Senator Cranston, Congress has the power to bring the executive branch up before you. You've got to take more than a
passive position." The room was growing heated.

HolLynn brought up the separate-but-equal issue. Daniel Yohalem of the Children's Defense Fund explained how the university consortium idea was a separate-but-equal system.

At this, Cranston frowned and said, "Separate but equal is not
acceptable."

He paused.

I held my breath.

He continued: "I cannot believe there is any deliberate desire
to continue discrimination. But I agree. Costs should not be an
issue here. I will make a statement. A consortium is not acceptable. That will be in my statement."

I let my breath out.

Then Frank Bowe stood up. Thirty years old, with intense
brown eyes, Frank had an innocent air about him. He looked
directly into Senator Cranston's eyes. Then he started signing,
while Lynette Taylor translated.

"Senator, we're not even second-class citizens."

Frank paused. His face showed weariness. "We're third-class citizens."

With his words, a profound feeling entered our bodies, weighing on us, pulling us down into our seats. Out of the blue, we knew: Frank is right. We are third-class citizens.

Suddenly we were all fighting back tears.

We were filthy, exhausted, and completely wrung out, and we were third-class citizens.

As we left Senator Cranston's office, he shook our hands.

WE HAD TO KEEP GOING. We rolled to Senator Harrison Williams's office. He stood attentively, his dark bushy eyebrows serious.

I was direct: "This is a request for another statement from you and for an audience with President Carter in cooperation with Senator Cranston."

We updated him on the regulations.

Senator Williams agreed to team up with Cranston and issue a statement. The meeting went very fast. Hale fell asleep halfway through. We were all so tired.

We went back to the church to regroup.

After our day of meetings on Capitol Hill, I got the feeling that people were starting to believe that we might win, but I was not there yet. I thought we were making progress, but I knew—from my time in Senator Williams's office, from my time as an activist, and just from my life—that things aren't over until they're over.

We spent the rest of the day working on getting a meeting with the White House. We called staffers, congressional representatives, basically anyone with power. Finally, we got a meeting for the next day with Carter's chief of domestic policy, Stuart E. Eizenstat—a coup.

In order for our meeting with Eizenstat to be constructive, we had to be sure that our scrappy and exhausted delegation of thirty-four spoke with one voice. We spent the night prepping our strategy. We went to bed very late.

The church wasn't really set up for sleeping, but we didn't care. Some of us slept in the pews and some on the floor of a big room used for hosting coffee receptions after church services. Everybody helped everybody with whatever they needed to get ready for bed, get up and down off the floors, and to the bathroom. After a few hours, we got up, had breakfast, and a small delegation of us went to the White House.

They held us up at reception and wouldn't let us in until we each swore that we would not start a sit-in in the White House. I couldn't hide the hint of a smile I felt curling across my face.

Stuart Eizenstat was a youngish man with neatly combed hair and tortoise-shell glasses. Frank Bowe opened the meeting and then I spoke, starting by stating my feelings about the mistreatment the DC protesters had suffered from the administration and discussing the history and weakening of the regulations. The rest of the delegation chimed in.

Eizenstat refused to take any responsibility for Califano's refusal to sign the regulations.

"We in the domestic policy staff coordinate to make sure the legislation we propose is consistent with the president's policy. We have not gotten involved with regulations before." In other words, it was a HEW issue, not a presidential issue.

Again, we responded.

"Section 504 is a major social change," Bruce Curtis pointed out.

"No other civil rights laws have had costs implied," I said, referring to the argument that Section 504 would cost too much to implement.

"The issue of not including drug and alcohol use is a red herring. Of course the regulations wouldn't include someone who is unable to work," Daniel Yohalem explained.

Taking notes, Eizenstat appeared to be listening carefully.

"With respect," I said, "we have the support of labor and other organizations of minority groups. The disability organizations are strong, and yet we feel we are being led around by the nose. Few other sets of regulations have had to go through the ordeal we have been led through. Nondisabled individuals are telling us they know best."

We requested a meeting with President Carter.

Finally, in a subtle and indirect way, Eizenstat made it clear that he believed it was time for the administration to act.

Then he left us with his deputy assistant of domestic affairs, Bert Carp. Neither man agreed to arrange a meeting with President Carter.

As the meeting ended, we asked Mr. Carp where we could find an accessible restroom. He had to go ask someone to find out and then came back to tell us that we had to actually leave the White House and cross the street to go to the New Executive Office building.

Afterward, we held a candlelight vigil outside the White House.

WHEN WE GOT BACK TO THE CHURCH, we all split up for a while. Some people went to dinner, others got a drink; I got on the phone. I tried to call CeCe and Ray in San Francisco, but they weren't answering. I was worried. Some reports had come through that the demonstrations in the Federal Building were starting to fray. After trying a few more times, I went to a bar with a few of the others. After an hour I went back to the church and tried to call the Federal Building again. CeCe answered, thank God. Everyone was holding strong, she reassured me, and I was very relieved. The protesters were all eager for information, she said. I gave her an update on everything that had happened that day and we hung up.

As a result, we weren't able to assemble in the church and start talking until ten o'clock that night.

Right away it emerged that most of the delegation wanted to go back to San Francisco. Given the way the meetings with Senator Cranston, Senator Williams, and Stuart Eizenstat had gone, they felt fairly certain the regulations were going to be signed. Some people talked about ending the demonstration, either by getting arrested or just declaring victory.

Kitty and I vehemently disagreed, as did a few others. The regulations were not yet signed, and I refused to give up until they were. Almost there is not there.

In the argument that ensued, the crevasses between the East and West Coast opened up. The East Coast protesters felt we were too confrontational and unwilling to compromise. This pushed my buttons.

"We have compromised throughout our whole lives," I said. Tears of frustration came to my eyes. Angrily I shook them away. "It is enough."

The West Coast leadership team was almost all women. Would we have been considered too confrontational and unwilling to compromise if we were men? I knew that was one of the underlying issues. Too strong and we were "aggressive"; too passive and we were "ineffective." I was very annoyed, but I didn't say it. I didn't want to create any more divisiveness. We *needed* to stay together. Fighting among ourselves was a sure way to fail.

"Why should we stop now when we're so close?" I asked.

But people were tired and wrung out. They wanted to go home.

Finally, we agreed to let the San Francisco protesters decide what to do. We got CeCe and Ray on the phone and explained what was happening. "Can you put it to the protesters?" we asked them. "Ask them to vote."

They called us back.

The protesters had voted to stay the course. The demonstration would continue.

It was five in the morning when we went to bed.

But still, I couldn't sleep.

I lay awake looking at the ceiling, reviewing every decision we'd made, getting more and more frustrated with Califano and Carter.

Carter had *campaigned* on a promise to us! We'd *worked* for him, supported his campaign.

Yet he was choosing money and convenience over us, over our civil rights. Over our humanity.

Everything was teetering, I could feel it. People were running dry. How much time did we have before it all fell apart?

When I saw Lynette pass by me, I decided to get up.

"Pssssst, can you help me get into my chair?" I whispered. Most of the delegation was still sleeping, but as Lynette helped me go to the bathroom a few others also got up.

I sat in my chair, thinking. It was getting warm in DC. I wiped my forehead. I was sweaty, I smelled terrible, and my hair was greasy. I was angry.

I just couldn't believe Califano was still ignoring us.

What the fuck did we have to do? This had to end now.

I looked around the church.

"Let's go try and meet with Califano," I said to everyone who was awake.

Ten of us loaded into the truck and drove to HEW.

The front of the building was glass doors, which were blocked by six tough-looking guards with billy clubs. We rolled up to the door. We were about to enter when a guard intercepted me.

"Sorry ma'am," he said. "You can't enter here."

"We're here to meet with Secretary Califano," I told him calmly. I was certain he must be confused. There was no way they could be blocking everyday citizens from entering the building. At that time security did not exist in the way it does now.

"Sorry, ma'am," he repeated. "I can't let you in."

"We're citizens," I told him with irritation. "We have the right to meet with Secretary Califano. Can I speak with your manager?"

"Sorry, ma'am," he repeated in the exact same tone for the third time. "I can't let you do that."

Gradually it dawned on me. They were refusing to allow us in. Not everyone. *Us.* They must have been under specific orders to watch out for people in wheelchairs trying to get into the building.

I felt like I'd been slapped across my face.

My jaw tightened.

How many times had I been blocked from going somewhere? Told I couldn't get in? Told "No, not you"?

Buses, planes, schools, restaurants, theaters, offices, friends' houses flashed through my mind.

I was sick of being *blocked*.

I didn't care if it was a guard, a bus driver, a pilot, a principal, a manager, or a step. It was all the same. They were all the same.

I looked up at the guard, fury in my eyes.

I turned around and backed up.

Then, I drove my chair directly toward the building. The guards jumped to the side and watched me, frozen in total disbelief, as I smashed into the door.

The others followed me in their chairs.

Over and over again, we turned around. *Smash, smash, smash.* We slammed into the doors.

The guards came alive. Armed and in uniform, they started holding our chairs.

LATER, WHEN I WAS INTERVIEWED about the incident, I said the truth. Secretary Califano is "arrogant, obstinate, and absolutely inhumane," I told a reporter. "The regulations are our lifeblood and he still refuses to even meet with us." In response, Califano's spokesperson claimed our charges relating to the 504 regulations were inaccurate.

That was Friday, April 23, the eighteenth day of the protest. We decided to hold a rally in front of the White House on the following Tuesday. Over the weekend we prepped, using the Machinists' headquarters as home base. We had to get people mobilized, figure out transportation, plan the agenda, invite speakers, and work the press. The organizing and coordination took a great deal of effort, but that wasn't what worried me the most. The thing that had me concerned was the growing conflict between the East and West Coast protesters. I could feel the heat of their disapproval. They didn't like our approach. But the lesson I had learned from my parents was embedded in my DNA:

If you believe in something, do whatever you have to do to get your point across.

When someone ignores you, it's an intentional display of power. They're essentially acting like you don't exist, and they do it because they can. They believe that nothing will happen to them. Ignoring silences people. It intentionally avoids resolution or compromise. It ignites your worst fears of unworthiness because it makes you feel that you *deserve* to be ignored. Inevitably, being ignored puts you in the position of having to choose between making a fuss or accepting the silent treatment. If you stand up to the ignorer and get in their face, you break the norms of polite behavior and end up feeling worse, diminished, demeaned.

This is what Califano was doing to us. And it was working.

It played on all of us.

ON SATURDAY NIGHT we left off our prepping for the rally to go to Califano's house again to hold another candlelight vigil. We were unloading from the truck, when Kitty's cousin Jimmy came out of his house to talk to the news reporters camped in front of Califano's house. He was mad.

Gesturing toward his mother's house, across the street from Califano's, he yelled, "This is my mother's house and she's ninety years old, and in a wheelchair, and she hasn't had a wink of sleep all night! What are these people doing?" Jimmy hadn't seen Kitty yet—clearly he hadn't made the connection between his cousin and our motley crew.

From where she was sitting, still inside the truck, Kitty heard his voice and panicked. Trying to hide, she pulled a blanket over her head. She stayed in the back of the truck for the entire vigil.

Califano ignored our vigil and, as we were to discover, left through his back door. Which is what he had apparently done the first morning we were there.

We decided to start using these backdoor exits against Califano—using them directly contradicted Carter's "Open Door Administration" slogan. We'd force him into situations where he would have to choose between speaking with us or leaving through a back door; then we'd point this out in the press.

The Sunday morning after our candlelight vigil in front of Califano's house, we picketed the front of President Carter's church, First Baptist.

He and Mrs. Carter saw us as they were going into the service, but afterward, he slipped out the back.

A reporter picked up on it. "Inside, President Carter taught his Bible class before hearing a sermon in which the pastor said, 'We can't dwell in comfort with poverty all around us.'"

In our next press release we wrote that we remained "stymied by the administration's new backdoor policy."

————

ON TUESDAY, the day of our demonstration in front of the White House, the sky was clear.

Our announcement to the press included five pages of endorsements, including from a governor, a mayor, and seven US members of Congress.

Dog-tired from sleeping on the church pews, we piled into the truck and drove to Lafayette Park in front of the White House, where we assembled a stage and a sound system. In the late morning, about a hundred protesters arrived. Simultaneously, our colleagues around the country were holding reinvigorated rallies in Dallas and Houston; Hartford, Connecticut; Eugene, Oregon; Kansas City, Missouri; and San Francisco and Los Angeles.

I opened the demonstration. A lengthy list of high-powered speakers followed me, from five US congressmen and a DC city councilwoman to our friends at the Machinists and the Arc of the United States. Bands played and we sang, with the sign language interpreters signing the words to the songs. People had protest signs such as "How can we get on the bandwagon when we can't get on the bus?" It was a last glorious coming together.

That night we decided to send most of the DC delegation home to San Francisco. The protesters in the building needed reinforcements and most people were ready to go home.

The next day, everyone left except six of us. Incredibly, Evan White and his cameraman stayed to keep following the story. We who stayed behind were not giving up on getting to Califano. We discovered that he was scheduled to give a talk at the National Press Club. We went to see if we could get him to talk to us.

AT THE NATIONAL Press Club they wouldn't allow us into the building, so we stayed outside and picketed. But because Evan White had press credentials the Press Club couldn't keep him out. Evan got into the briefing, where he tried to ask Califano some questions about the sit-in, but Califano refused to call on him.

Afterward, Evan and his cameraman broke White House protocol by following Califano out of the room to ask questions. Califano's guards blocked Evan from following Califano into the elevator, but then the elevator car accidentally returned to where Evan was standing and the door opened. Pushing the microphone into Califano's face while his cameraman filmed, Evan asked Califano a series of questions through the door.

"What is the status on the 504 regulations? Will you sign the regulations as they were drafted?"

Califano refused to respond, but the cameraman captured all of it.

Evan reported the incident on the television news, adding that Califano had yet again escaped through a back door.

After that incident, everyone became certain that Califano was going to sign the regulations. Everyone, that is, except me.

I thought Califano might be very likely to sign now, but not signed was not signed. I wasn't going to trust that he wouldn't try to wriggle out of it again.

So when the rest of the protesters decided to return to the Federal Building in San Francisco that same day, I stayed on in DC with Pat Wright.

The next day Pat and I were sitting in a bar on Capitol Hill, watching the news and talking about what to do next, when a reporter came on. The reporter said that Joseph Califano, secretary of the US Department of Health, Education, and Welfare, had signed the enabling regulations for Section 504 of the Rehabilitation Act of 1973 as they'd been written under the Ford administration.

It was Thursday, April 28, the twenty-fourth day of the sit-in.

Pat and I looked at each other. Was it true? We couldn't believe it.

But it was true.

I was told that there was jubilation on the fourth floor of the San Francisco Federal Building—victorious shouting, hugging, laughter, and, ultimately, crying.

Because, as it turned out, people didn't want to leave the building.

They'd made friends, had fun, fallen in love, and felt fully free to be themselves. And in the process, something magical had happened. In the cocoon of the building, a metamorphosis had occurred.

"We all feel in love with each other," CeCe Weeks explained to a reporter.

"I've discovered that I count as a person," a protester told another reporter.

"Instead of seeing myself as a weak person, I found my strength reinforced by others like me," said another.

"I'm going to miss them," said a Federal Building guard; he had started learning sign language and hoped one day to become a sign language interpreter. "They were real nice people."

Nobody expected to feel as heartbroken as they did that the sit-in was ending.

They decided to spend one last night together in the building, to celebrate.

ON THE MORNING of Saturday, April 30, twenty-six days after the first rally outside the Federal Building, over one hundred validated protesters left the building for the last time. Hugging and kissing the guards, singing "We Have Overcome," smiling and waving, holding "Victory" signs, carrying plastic crates, backpacks, and bags of belongings, they emerged into the sunlight of the plaza in a long line.

Outside, an exuberant crowd waited for them, clapping, holding signs, smiling, and chanting, "Power to the people."

PART THREE

BERKELEY, CALIFORNIA

1981

CHAPTER 9

THE RECKONING

FOR US AT the Center for Independent Living in Berkeley, the years following the signing of the 504 regulations were a chaotic time. Getting a law passed doesn't necessarily make it happen. In 1956, when the Supreme Court ordered the city of Montgomery, Alabama, to desegregate in the wake of the bus boycott, the buses didn't have to be redesigned before the law could be implemented. But with disability, even though 504 had been passed and the regulations signed, structural changes had to be made to allow us access, and structural change requires commitment and effort. To ensure that Section 504 would be understood, implemented, and enforced, projects, programs, and organizations had to be formed.

Many didn't want to do what it took to integrate the schools, or make buildings accessible, or do any of the myriad other things that the regulations required. The American Public Transit Association put out a letter saying it was going to cost much too much money to make the bus system accessible. So we geared up for a big fight and discovered that it cost the same amount of money to put air conditioning in a bus as it did to put in a wheelchair lift. The bus association's financial model had been erroneously based on the idea that most disabled people wouldn't use the bus, which was a huge presumption. Yes, I was fearful when I first started using the bus, because I didn't know how a city bus would work with my wheelchair, but once I practiced I got comfortable and started using it all the time.

The truth is, the status quo loves to say no. It is the easiest thing in the world to say no, especially in the world of business and finance. But for the first time we were discussing civil rights, and no other civil rights issue has ever been questioned because of the cost.

In the aftermath of 504, the challenge—or the opportunity, depending on how you look at it—was on us, the disability advocates and allies who had fought so hard for the regulations to be signed. We had to challenge the nos by working on solutions. When ridiculous statements were made, we had to respond. We needed to help people see that when the barriers were removed, everyone would benefit. This meant that we had to anticipate what the nos were going to be, develop arguments against them, and create answers that people couldn't say no to.

One of the simplest arguments against change is to say that something is too expensive, unsafe, or impossible. Saying something is expensive, unsafe, or impossible pushes you down a rabbit warren of arguments. It forces you to discuss various interpretations of multiple financial and safety scenarios—and it distracts from the issue that when something is a civil right we must have ingenuity. People need to assume that it is possible to figure things out, that we can problem-solve and act.

We—the disability activists—had to do what we could to be prepared to provide technical assistance, to speak with and, when necessary, argue with the engineers and financial analysts. As a result, activists started to pursue their studies and specialize. This was a huge boost to our momentum.

At the same time, we had to recognize that, when change occurs, it's natural for people to be on a learning curve. We had to help people get past their somewhat automatic mental block against being able to see life as a disabled person. Telling stories allowed people to begin to see things through our eyes.

The '70s, essentially, sparked a huge churning of the wheels.

On our side, we had to shore our people up so they would be prepared to take on the nos. The nature of antidiscrimination laws is that they only get enforced when someone makes a complaint. In other words, if an institution doesn't voluntarily comply with the law and violates your civil right, the only way to address it is to submit a complaint. And submitting a complaint, fighting a court case, looking someone in the eye and saying, "You're wrong," is intimidating. We struggle with the assumption that institutions know more than we do, because that is what we're taught.

Remember what I told you about being given the implicit message that my needs were a burden to others? People with disabilities also have to work to overcome the feeling that asking for an equal opportunity is asking for too much.

Part of the problem is that we tend to think that equality is about treating everyone the same, when it's not. It's about fairness. It's about equity of access. And equity of access, whether to housing, health, education, or employment, looks different for someone like me and the hundreds of thousands of us who cannot do things the same way, than it does for the majority of people who can. It involves ramps, wider doorways, bars, sign language interpreters, captioning, accessible technology, audio descriptions, documents in Braille, and personal assistance for those with physical disabilities, as well as those with intellectual disabilities.

When this is not understood, we get framed as "complaining" and "selfish," even though we're simply asking for the same rights as everyone else. This especially happens to women. We're called

"demanding," and if we refuse to back down, we're "relentless."
But labeling us "demanding" and "relentless" is just a different
way of trying to make us "submit."

How did we shore people up? Well, CIL was run by people
with disabilities, so the simple act of doing our day-to-day work
was empowering to ourselves and the disabled people we worked
with. But we also offered programs. For people who were living
in more restrictive environments—who were perhaps feeling
dependent and out of control of their lives—we connected them
with people who were living more independently in the community. This helped people get clearer about who they were and
what they wanted, so they would have the confidence to speak
up for themselves. If you're going to look a naysayer in the face
and tell them they're wrong, or stand up and demand your civil
or human rights, you'd better be clear about who you are and
what you want.

With antidiscrimination laws, when a complaint is submitted it may be followed by a court case where the final result is
based on the ruling of a judge. If a judge is not sympathetic, or
the law is not clear or comprehensive enough, the result can be
negative. Complaints were being brought to courts, and judges
were making widely different rulings, some clearly going against
the spirit of 504. Just as there were people who didn't want the
race divide to end, there were people who didn't want the disability divide to end. Frankly, many people don't necessarily see
racial or disability segregation as having an adverse effect on their
communities or schools. In fact, some people don't *want* to live
in communities where everyone is included. There's a "Not in
my neighborhood, not in my school, not in my restaurant" kind
of sentiment. Until fairly recently, different cities had "ugly laws"
on the books that prohibited disabled people from begging; it
was called "unsightly begging," that is, it exposed their "diseased,
maimed, mutilated, or . . . deformed" body in public for profit.[1]

In order to fight the necessary legal battles, CIL started the Disability Law Resource Center, which then became the Disability Rights Education and Defense Fund (DREDF) and got spun out of CIL as its own entity. At DREDF, as my old friend Mary Lou Breslin, who was one of the DREDF founders, would later say, "The phones never stopped ringing. You couldn't walk two feet without tripping over somebody or something, whether a dog, a cane, or a wheelchair." It was the first civil rights legal organization run by and for people with disabilities, and people were calling from all over the country and the world, wanting information on issues. A slow reckoning was happening.

For the first few years I was at CIL overseeing much of the work. The year 1981 was designated the International Year of the Disabled Person, and that, combined with the sit-in and signing of 504, had made us a topic of great interest to our activist colleagues abroad. People from other countries wanted to see what we were doing, and what had led to such massive demonstrations. The BBC filmed a segment on us, as did a team of Japanese filmmakers, and the Canadian Broadcasting Corporation. I relished the opportunity to connect with people globally. Being the daughter of German immigrants and having been raised in immigrant Brooklyn had always made me feel very aware of the rest of the world.

My first trip to Europe became a trip of many firsts for me. With my brother and a couple of friends I went to Germany. No one in my family had been to Germany since my parents had left as kids. We knew the idea of visiting would open up memories of a very painful, terrible time for my parents, so before we made any plans my brother and I asked their permission. My father connected us with an old friend of his. The man picked us up and took us to see where my father had grown up, in Hoffenheim. The people, none of whom were Jews, were very kind to us.

But the remarkable thing was this: Not one word was said about what had happened to the Jews. Even when they took us to my father's old house and showed us pictures of my father and his brothers. Even when they showed us the site where the synagogue had been burned down.

What a pervasive influence silence and avoidance have had on my life.

Why wasn't I in school?

Silence.

Why aren't we allowed on buses?

Silence.

Why can't disabled people teach?

Silence.

Where are all the Jews going?

Piercing silence.

I refuse to give in to the pressure of the silence.

This is one of the things about me. I persist. I insist on speaking. On being heard.

In Germany, I went to the Paralympics and for the first time met disabled people from South America and Africa and all over the world. What surprised me the most was the level of disparities that existed. For the first time I was being exposed to the great inequality between the rich nations of the world and the poor nations of the world. Even among the Paralympians, who are among the elite athletes of their countries, there was tremendous disparity.

After Germany I went to Sweden on a program where I got to learn about Sweden's social welfare system—and how it provided financial security, healthcare, and social services, protecting Swedish society. This opened my eyes to the fact that how we did things in the US was not the norm everywhere.

My entire trip had a profound impact on me. It made me see things in a different way than I had before.

After 504, as an increasing number of international visitors came to CIL and we got more invitations to go abroad, I got excited about the idea of working globally.

At heart I am a networker and a convener. I meet people and introduce them to other people. I suck up as much information as I can and try to share it with as many people as I can. In my travels I'd been developing a small nucleus of international disabled activists who also became my friends. Kalle Konkkola was a young Finnish activist who used a motorized wheelchair, and Adolf Ratzka was a young German activist who also used a motorized wheelchair. Kalle and Adolf, like Ed, used mechanical ventilation to breath. We were all unique for the times: We were disabled *and* we'd gone to college. We'd challenged the system that said how we had to be taken care of and had turned it on its head. We weren't ashamed of who we were and what we needed and we were no longer willing to let charity organizations, focused on finding a "cure," speak for us. Each working in our own respective countries, together we pushed to change the conversation to one of equality and rights instead of cures.

In my work in the US, I began to see the issue of disability rights around the world as our next frontier.

In 1980, Ed and I and another colleague, Joan Leon, cofounded the World Institute on Disability (WID). The three of us became the codirectors of the organization. WID was a global think tank. We researched global disability issues, studied other countries, influenced the development of programs and policies, and collaborated with disability leaders around the world.

Right away, it was the countries with universal healthcare that impressed me the most, the way their concept of healthcare extended far beyond our idea of healthcare. For example, they included personal assistance under the concept of healthcare, with the thought that help getting dressed, going shopping, cooking, and so forth was an essential part of someone's well-being and should be covered. But it didn't stop there. In some countries, housing authorities received money to work with people to modify their houses or apartments and make them accessible, whether they rented or owned.

I remember a friend from Australia staying with me in my house in Berkeley. I lived in a rented house where I couldn't use the bathroom to wash my hair, which meant I had to wash my hair in the kitchen sink. My friend, truly puzzled, asked why I didn't make my bathroom more accessible. She just had no idea that there was no money available in the US to do anything like that.

What was different about the US, on the other hand, was the level of advocacy. People in the States, disabled or not, just seemed much more driven to advocate for change. My feeling was that we saw our role with government very differently than people in other countries. We spent enormous time and energy trying to influence policy.

This was something that people from abroad were very interested in learning about—how *were* we getting civil rights laws like 504 passed and implemented?

Our peers from Europe complained about how their barriers were seen as purely medical, rather than an issue of human or civil rights. The basic question was about autonomy. Disabled people wanted to be able to live where they wished, get up and eat when they wished, and hire the personal assistants who helped them, provided they complied with laws regarding workers' rights and benefits, of course. When these supports were run from a medical approach they didn't necessarily support a person's ability to be autonomous, which is why our concept of independent living was so important—and starting to permeate other countries' thinking.

We started getting grants to compare state policies to the policies of specific European countries, developed an internship program, and organized the first conference on aging and disability. We were concerned that the structures being set up for older people replicated the same segregation that young people were experiencing. For the first time we started to talk about aging in terms of what people wanted their future to look like if they acquired a disability, because everyone wants autonomy, regardless of age. We gained ideas and became knowledgeable enough to influence policy.

And this is how I discovered that no other country had an antidiscrimination law like 504.

SECTION 504 HAD REDEFINED DISABILITY. Instead of looking at disability as a medical issue, it had made disability a question of civil—and human—rights. This was the difference my friends from abroad were talking about.

In traveling around the world with WID, I came to understand that we—Kitty and I and Pat and Joni and Mary Lou and Mary Jane and Jim and Eunice and Frank and all the other protesters who had given up so much to get 504 signed—had done something momentous.

People have asked me, "Were you angry?" Was I angry about all the barriers, all the violations, all the mistreatment I've lived through? Is that what fueled my activism? I feel sometimes that that question is tinged with an unspoken judgment. As women, we are taught that anger is somehow wrong.

A COUPLE OF YEARS after we started WID, Joan called me. It was a sunny Berkeley afternoon and I was at my desk in my bedroom.

"Judy," Joan said, "the board has decided that they don't want WID to have three codirectors." Joan was using a matter-of-fact tone of voice, but clearly she was not happy. My stomach dropped.

"What?"

I couldn't think.

"They're making Ed the sole director of WID. We're going to be beneath him."

"But there's been no process. They've just made this decision? They're not even going to talk to us?" I just couldn't believe what Joan was saying.

"They've just decided. They don't want to have a discussion about it."

We hung up.

I was very hurt. I knew Joan felt as bad as I did but I also knew her circumstances were different. Joan was a nondisabled person in a disability movement and as such she didn't expect to play the lead role.

I needed time to think.

I'd known that the board didn't like the codirector structure and was going to talk about what to do about it. But there'd been no discussion with us at all. No information about any kind of process, no understanding of how the decision was going to be made. The men on the board, and it was mostly men, had simply made a decision.

The thing is, I thought, maybe they were right. Ed was well known and "famous" in a way that I wasn't. He also knew more people in California and had more relationships, which was important for funding and many other things. And Ed could go out there and do or say anything.

Although, I now think, looking back, that I could too. Albeit in a different way.

The truth was, I didn't push myself forward in the same way Ed did. Ed did it naturally. He presumed things would open up, that he would be welcomed. He presumed privilege. For me, it was something I had to work on. I never felt like I could presume acceptance of my ideas, of myself. I found myself being deferential to men, even when I didn't mean to be.

When I was growing up, men were expected to be the head of the household.

In our synagogue in Brooklyn where my father carried me up the stairs, the men sat up front and the women sat in the back. Only men received the aliyah, which is when you enter the bimah, the platform where the Torah is read, to recite a blessing before and after a reading of the Torah. Women didn't enter the bimah or receive the aliyah.

Growing up, I lived two truths: My mother was a fighter. And my mother deferred to my father.

I'd been taught to do whatever it took to get my point across, to question authority, to stand up for myself.

And I'd been raised to be a good girl.

In Berkeley, I went to a new synagogue and, after making the bimah accessible for me, the rabbi asked me if I would receive the aliyah. Oh my god, I thought, I've never been asked to do an aliyah.

I learned how to do it.

Let me be clear. I was proud to work with Ed. He did fantastic things. At fourteen he'd transitioned from being a totally independent, athletic teenager to being dependent on help to live—and he'd emerged as a fighter and a visionary. He had an inner strength and a manner that enabled all people to feel that they made a difference in this world. People loved and admired Ed for his tenacity and his beautiful smile.

Ed made people believe that all things were possible. We were very fond of each other. We were like brother and sister. I believe we strengthened each other.

Ed changed my life. It was because of Ed that I came to Berkeley in the first place, and then came back to Berkeley from Washington. Ed and I and Joan had started WID together.

At the same time, as a man, Ed could get things wrong, repeat himself, and make promises he couldn't keep.

And Ed would still be in charge.

As women, we could say all the right things, do a thousand things correctly, and follow through on all our commitments.

We could lead a hundred and fifty people to take over the Federal Building in San Francisco and change the laws for disabled people.

But we were not in charge.

People called me pushy.

People never called Ed pushy.

This affected me. Of course my women friends in California were on me about it. But I was always walking a tightrope. And I had to grow, internally, as we all do. As disabled women, we didn't have help from the women's movement. We were always pushing to have our issues considered and supported by the women's movement, but we were largely ignored.

We were basically on our own.

So let me answer the earlier question: Was I angry? And I will tell you that yes, I was angry. I have, in fact, been filled with rage at times. Some of those times I have spoken of, such as when I snarled traffic on Madison Avenue at rush hour with my wheelchair and my group from Disabled in Action, or slammed my wheelchair into the glass doors that were closed to us at HEW, but I have not been able to tell you every single story.

But, is this anger wrong? Is it unladylike and selfish, as we were taught to believe when I was young? I believe not.

Our anger was a fury sparked by profound injustices. Wrongs that deserved ire.

And with that rage we ripped a hole in the status quo.

I WAS AT WID when the work on the Americans with Disabilities Act started.

We'd been talking about the fact that 504 covered only the public sector and eventually, sooner rather than later, we would need a national piece of legislation that prohibited discrimination in the private sector as well. Basically, since we'd been left out of the Civil Rights Act of 1964, we needed our own Civil Rights Act. Around 1980, we started coming together to make the case for the legislation.

As I mentioned, Mary Lou Breslin went on from the sit-in to cofound the newly formed DREDF, along with Pat Wright, another one of the sit-in leaders, Bob Funk, and a civil rights lawyer by the name of Arlene Mayerson. DREDF was integral to the development of and ultimate passage of the ADA.

The campaign to pass the ADA was a completely different process than what happened with 504. Whereas section 504 was a sleeper that got snuck in stealthily as an addition to a different law, the ADA, an expansion of 504, came in through the front door. It's hard for us now to imagine Republicans and Democrats coming together to solve a major societal issue, but this is exactly what happened with the ADA.

In 1981, Ronald Reagan appointed a wonderful man named Justin Dart to the newly formed National Council on Disability (NCD).

Justin Dart was a Republican. A successful entrepreneur who'd had polio and used a wheelchair, Justin came from a wealthy Republican family in Chicago. He always wore a cowboy hat and cowboy boots. He was very respectful of everyone and so he was respected by everyone. Justin was zealous about civil rights and had been active on disability rights in Texas and abroad.

On the NCD, one of the first things Justin did was figure out a way to connect with disability activists in the United States. He traveled around the country and met with local disability leaders, getting their feedback, and buy-in, on the creation of a national policy for civil rights for people with disabilities. At that time traveling with a disability was expensive and complicated, so the fact that Justin did this—at his own expense—was extraordinary.

Not long after Justin's trip, he and Lex Friedan, the director of the NCD, and Bob Burgdorf, a lawyer for the NCD, wrote the first draft of a national policy on disability. This draft, which was based on the feedback Justin had gathered on his trip, was met with a rather lukewarm response on the part of the Republican members appointed to the council. Until, that is, Joseph Dusenbury, the chair of the council and director of the South Carolina Vocational Rehabilitation Agency, stood up. Standing in front of the council he waited for silence before speaking.

"Ladies and gentlemen," he said, "this document was written by the disabled people of the United States. I want to hear a motion to approve this document and I don't want you to change a single word."[2]

You must know that despite all our advances, actually asking disabled people what *they* wanted and talking about disability as a civil rights issue was still a radical concept at that time. Later, partially as a result of his standing by his principles, Joseph Dusenbury would lose his position as chair of the NCD.

But now the council approved the document. A meeting was convened of people from across the country to discuss the proposed draft, in which I participated, which kicked off a series of serious discussions about a national disability policy.

From that point on, the movement for the ADA grew rapidly; but simultaneously, a movement was mounted against us.

The anti-ADA movement came from many directions.

Businesses were fighting, worried what the ADA might cost, in time and money.

President Reagan was trying to weaken many of the regulations related to IDEA, the education act for disabled children, the law I'd worked on when I was in Senator Williams's office.

And institutions were fighting the 504 regulations in court. One of the most famous cases, *Southeastern Community College v. Davis*, was brought by a community college nursing program that had denied entrance to a deaf woman. The Supreme Court found that Davis's hearing impairment rendered her unqualified to participate in the program. The decision, which was based on a very negative interpretation of Section 504, cast doubt on how accommodation for the needs of disabled people would be interpreted in the future.

DREDF fought back.

A new case came before the Supreme Court in 1984, *Consolidated Rail Corporation v. Darrone*. It raised the question of how employment discrimination was covered by the antidiscrimination provisions of Section 504. DREDF upped the ante on the case and collected testimony from sixty-three national, state, and local organizations, filing an amicus brief that not only educated the courts on employment discrimination but also demonstrated to the court, beyond any doubt, that this issue concerned millions of Americans. DREDF also worked very closely with the lawyer representing the disabled person in the lawsuit.

The court ruled in our favor. And, equally important, the court found that the 504 regulations, for which we'd fought so hard, were entitled to great deference by the courts.

It was an enormous victory.

It was the 504 regulations, elevated by the court in the *Consolidated Rail Corporation* case, which would form the basis of the ADA.

In the meantime, Justin, Lex, and Bob were building the case for support in Congress, which takes time. In 1986, the NCD officially arrived at the conclusion that disability discrimination was one of the most significant problems faced by disabled people. Backed by testimony from thousands of people, they submitted a report titled *Toward Independence* to President Reagan, and Congress that recommended passage of a comprehensive law requiring equal opportunity for people with disabilities.

The response from the White House shows just how radical this was.

A key member of the White House staff called Justin.

"What were you folks thinking about with this civil rights thing?" the staff person said. "The President won't touch it with a ten-foot pole. Take it out [of the report]."[3]

Justin refused to back down. He met with the assistant attorney general for civil rights, Bradford Reynolds.

"Bradford," he said in his characteristically direct way, "I do not believe that Ronald Reagan wants to go down in history as the president who opposed keeping the promise of the Declaration of Independence to thirty-five million Americans with disabilities."[4]

After a significant silence, Bradford committed to getting the president's endorsement of the report, and Ronald Reagan did indeed endorse it.

So Justin Dart, Lex Friedan, and Bob Burgdorf were standing up to the president and Congress; DREDF and the other disability rights organizations were battling in court; and the disability activists were mobilizing—organizing protests and huge letter-writing campaigns.

Activists with ADAPT, an organization that started in 1983 to protest inaccessible transportation, were stopping buses, propelling themselves out of their wheelchairs, and dragging themselves up the steps of buses.

Although I didn't live in Washington, I supported the work from my position at WID in California. I attended meetings, testified at hearings, and lobbied.

IN APRIL 1988 the first version of the Americans with Disabilities Act was introduced to Congress by Republican senator Lowell Weicker and Democratic congressman Tony Coelho.

Because most people still had little awareness of disability as an issue, Congressman Major Owens of New York created a congressional task force to gather information and present recommendations on the proposed ADA to Congress. He named Justin Dart cochair.

Justin took his appointment as an opportunity to unify the disability movement by making diverse appointments to the task force, including people who were HIV-positive. This was controversial.

"We should not have representatives of people with AIDS," he was told. "People with AIDS will die." To which Justin responded, "Of course they will die. So will you and I. We are not into perpetuating paternalism."[5]

He hit the road again. Again paying out of his own pocket, Justin reached thousands of people and filed thousands of petitions and statements about people's experiences of discrimination because of their disability.

The first version of ADA failed to pass Congress, but the education and awareness-raising continued, which was strategic on the part of the activists.

In September 1988 a joint hearing was held on Capitol Hill before the Senate Subcommittee on Disability Policy and the House Subcommittee on Select Education.

Seven hundred people attended—blind people, deaf people, parents of people with disabilities, people with HIV infection. I testified at the hearing, along with many others. It was at that hearing that Senator Edward Kennedy, Senator Harkin, and Representative Owens made the commitment to make bringing a comprehensive disability civil rights bill to the 1989 Congress a top priority,[6] supporting the work begun by Congressman Coelho and Senator Weicker. Three of these legislators had a personal connection with disability: Senator Kennedy's sister

Rosemary had cognitive disabilities; Tom Harkin had a brother who was deaf; and Tony Coelho himself suffered from epilepsy.

On May 9, 1989, Senators Harkin and David Durenberger introduced another version of the ADA to the Senate; Congressmen Coelho and Hamilton Fish simultaneously introduced the legislation to the House of Representatives.

By that time it had been eight years since Justin Dart had first traveled the country meeting with activists.

The bill was radical and would produce critical change. Its wording mandated that within two years of passage, everything would have to be accessible. Everything.

REMEMBER THAT I MENTIONED, during the sit-in, that Pat Wright's emergence as a brilliant strategist would have a big impact later?

Pat led the disability activist groups. United, they went full bore, gathering testimony on discrimination and lobbying Congress. Pat was called the General. One of the most significant things she did was to establish a partnership with traditional civil rights groups through the Leadership Conference on Civil Rights. There were negotiations and conversations, teams of lawyers, advocates, and policy analysts. A grassroots lobbying system was created, and more witnesses testified. Task forces were formed, networks were established. There were a multitude of hearings. At each one, witness after witness spoke about their experience with disability.

Thirty-six million Americans were finally being given the chance to speak.

Finally, on September 7, 1989, the ADA passed the Senate.

But then it got stuck in committee hearings in the House of Representatives.

For months. Six months.

Now, you might be wondering: Was this lengthy, very slow process driving us crazy? Were we planning on doing anything

to speed it up? Why didn't we, for example, haul our asses down
to the Capitol Building and sit in again? Force Congress to shift
into high gear?

Well, up until the point it got stuck in the House committees,
it hadn't been driving me crazy and I will tell you why: democracy is slow. The work of a democratic government is supposed
to be long and slow and hard. It must be that way.

Because the whole point of a democratic government is to
create laws and processes that allow some specific people to govern everyone else according to a previously-agreed-upon set of
contracts, so that we can live peaceably together in large groups,
meaningfully pursuing our lives—instead of living like Vikings,
marauding and pillaging, with the strongest tribe in charge. In order to work, a democracy needs checks and balances, thoughtful
deliberations, analysis, negotiation, and compromise. This is what
helps to prevent the people in whom we have invested power
from pulling fast ones, or simply making hasty bad decisions.

So, no, I was not too upset about the slow pace. Government
was doing its part. And we were doing our part as activists—
staying on top of government, tracking, keeping people accountable and honest. As long as we felt like everyone was working in
good faith, listening, and inviting the voice of the people into the
conversation, we felt the process was working as it should. It was
working for us the way it worked for everyone else.

It was when it got to the eleventh hour and the decision was
held up in House committees that we got angry. We worried that
the delaying tactics were a response to lobbying from the powerful entities of the anti-movement.

Which pissed us off.

On March 12, 1990, a thousand people came to Washington
to protest the failure of the government to pass the ADA.

In Washington, DC, the Lincoln Memorial is at one end of
the long grassy park that is the National Mall. At the other end is

the Capitol, home of the US Congress, the seat of power of the legislative branch.

At over two hundred eighty feet high, the Capitol is impressive. With its classical design harkening back to ancient Greece and Rome, it is one of the most recognizable symbols of representative democracy in the world.

To reach the Capitol's main entrance there are eighty-three marble steps to climb.

It was in front of those steps, on an unseasonably hot day in early spring, that the protesters who had come to Washington assembled. Pushing themselves out of their wheelchairs, dropping their crutches to the side, leaving any other mobility assistance behind, they began to climb the steps. Some landed softly with help from friends; while others fell out of their chairs directly onto the bottom step.

One by one, people dragged themselves up to the second, the third, the fourth step. Some inching forward on their backs, others lying on their bellies, their bodies and legs trailing behind. Using an elbow, a knee, a shoulder, they pulled themselves up.

One was a little girl named Jennifer Keelan. Jennifer, who had cerebral palsy, had come all the way to DC from Arizona after being denied service in a restaurant. "No one wants to watch you all eat," a waitress had told her. She'd become an activist and was determined to join the protest on the Capitol's marble steps.[7]

She used her elbows and knees to climb. Lying on her stomach on the second step, she raised her head to look at the stairs above her, her lip bloodied from where she had fallen on the hard marble. She was already sweating, a red, white, and blue bandanna tied around her head. Pausing, she asked for water, which several volunteers immediately offered.

It could take all night for her and the rest of the protesters to get to the top. Over sixty people climbed the steps.

"Two centuries is long enough for people with disabilities to wait before the constitutional promise of justice is kept," Justin had said at the rally, before the protesters started climbing.

Nine long years had passed since Justin first toured the country, and the protesters were forcing Congress to look at the indignity that they were forced to live with every single day, in a country that refused to end the segregation of and discrimination against people with disabilities. The next day the *Los Angeles Times* reported on the event and quoted Representative Patricia Schroeder:

> What we did for civil rights in the 1960s we forgot to do for people with disabilities.[8]

Four months later, the US House of Representatives finally passed the Americans with Disabilities Act.

JULY 26, 1990, was a glorious summer day in Washington, DC. The trees were lush, the sun was out, and the sky was blue. Three thousand people were gathered on the South Lawn of the White House. In front, standing on a platform, was President George H. W. Bush, with Justin Dart at his side. As President Bush began to speak, a hush fell on the enormous crowd.

"Let the shameful wall of exclusion finally come tumbling down," he said.

And he sat down at a desk and signed the Americans with Disabilities Act into law.

Our time had come. After nearly twenty years of protesting—from one coast to the other, under five presidents, Republican and Democratic—we had created what I believe to be the strongest, most comprehensive civil rights legislation for disability in the world.

I was forty-one years old, and, finally, I was an equal citizen.

Maybe what happened next wasn't an accident.

CHAPTER 10

CHINGONA

HE HAD VERY BROAD SHOULDERS. I noticed him immediately. As I maneuvered my chair over the grass, I kept my eye on him. He was sitting near a picnic table in a small cluster of people. It was a cool breezy August evening in Eugene, Oregon, and we were at a barbecue in someone's backyard. I'd flown from Berkeley to lead some workshops at my friend Susie Sygall's leadership retreat for disabled people. This particular group was from Mexico.

I watched as he moved his wheelchair through the group, laughing, relaxed. His hair was black and wavy.

"He's cute," I whispered to my friend Maribel. I was forty-two.

A year earlier I'd been with my father, talking about life, and men. My father, who was never scared, was scared. His cancer had spread.

"What kind of man are you looking for?" he'd asked me that day. I gave him my usual list of attributes and he just looked at me. I guess I sounded way too specific and closed-minded. Then he replied with one of his cryptic trademark parables: "Your mother-in-law hasn't been born yet." In other words, I needed to open my mind.

My dad died not long after that conversation.

———

I WENT OVER to the man and introduced myself. It was easy because I was working. I was supposed to be connecting with the workshop participants.

We sat together at a picnic table and talked. I didn't speak Spanish, but Maribel helped interpret. We'd been to a farm and a horse had accidentally bitten my finger. He looked at it and took my hand gently, asking me what I'd done to take care of the bite. His name was Jorge.

Maribel enlisted Susie to help interpret, and they were like schoolgirls egging me on, pushing us together at lunch the next day. Jorge's manner made the conversation flow easily. I discovered that as part of the delegation, he was helping a person who had cerebral palsy with some personal assistance. He had acquired his disability, which affected his ability to walk, at birth. He'd walked with braces and crutches in Mexico, but used a wheelchair in the US.

That night I invited him to come onto the bus with us on the way to the restaurant. Maribel and Susie tried to get me to sit separately with him to have dinner, just the two of us. But I was, like, "No way," so the four of us had dinner together. That was when I learned about how he'd met Gaby Brimmer, a disability rights activist in Mexico who had cerebral palsy, and quit his job as an accountant to work with her. He was funny and kind.

On the way back, we ended up on the same accessible bus. When Susie offered the little guest house in her backyard, Jorge and I spent the night together.

INSTEAD OF FLYING back to Mexico, he came to Berkeley and spent two weeks with me. We learned more about each other in that way that you do early in a new relationship. In a mixture of broken English, looked-up Spanish words, and signals, we traded stories and histories, views and beliefs, reveling in that euphoria of newness. He was eight years younger than me and came from a big family in Mexico City, for whom he had a great love. I learned about his deep connection to animals and the environment. I admired his strong values and principles.

A month later, he came back to Berkeley again. Six months later, he moved in with me.

We got married in Berkeley the following May. It was 1992.

In Berkeley, Jorge got a job and made new friends. We had a good life and it was a fun time for us. I was still at WID and we were in midst of the disability activists community in California. We talked about having kids. I was forty-four.

I WAS IN MY office at WID, a windowless room that gave no hint of the clear blue sky outside, when the phone rang. I picked it up to hear the familiar voice of a friend in Arkansas. After a few of the usual brief pleasantries, he cut to the chase and asked me a question I never expected to hear.

"Would you be interested in a role in the Bill Clinton administration?"

I was speechless.

I listened to him talk about what the Clinton administration was looking for and why he thought I'd be great. As he spoke, though, my mind filled with thoughts and questions. I was flattered, for sure. But I was happy with my life in Berkeley, happy with Jorge, happy with *our* life. Did I want to trade that relative calm for a ride on a political roller coaster? On the other hand, this was an opportunity to get into the driver's seat for a change, rather than always being the one fighting to just get on the bus. My mind buzzed. Before I realized what I was saying, almost instinctively, the words tumbled out of my mouth.

"I'd be interested in the assistant secretary position in the Office of Special Education and Rehabilitative Services in the Department of Education. And nothing else."

We talked a bit more and then hung up.

Turning my wheelchair around, I looked at the walls of my office. I couldn't believe what had just happened.

I WAS VERY FAMILIAR with the Office of Special Education and Rehabilitative Services, or OSERS, as we called it.

OSERS had been created in 1980 when HEW had been divided into the Department of Education and the US Department of Health and Human Services. It brought under one umbrella special education, rehabilitation services, and research. When I was at WID we'd been successful at getting a number of important grants from OSERS that had enabled us to advance our work as a public policy think tank.

And now I had just said that I wanted to lead it.

I was asked to interview for the position, which made me very nervous. At that point I had never in my life interviewed for a job. To get my teaching job I'd had to pass exams, but there'd been no face-to-face interview. I'd gotten my job at CIL because Ed, the board, and the staff knew me. And I was one of the three founders of WID. To make matters worse, I was supposed to be interviewed by two former governors, Secretary Richard Riley, former governor of South Carolina, and Deputy Secretary Madeleine Kunin, former governor of Vermont.

I managed to pull myself together for the interview. Which I probably owe to all my practice with the media, and all the times I'd had to think on my butt, as it were, under pressure.

"How'd it go?" Jorge asked me when I got home.

"Okay," I said. "But I was nervous. I kept wondering if they were thinking I wouldn't be able to do it because of my disability."

Although I did feel that the interviewers and I had ended up on the same page.

Not too long after, I was offered the position.

The only problem was, I was apprehensive.

I wasn't worried about whether or not I could actually do the job. I felt confident that I had enough experience. I'd gone through the special education and rehabilitation system and had been interacting with it my whole life. I had a good understanding of the issues OSERS dealt with, and I felt sure I could put together a good team and, along with the community, figure out the rest. I was concerned about other things, like, would I, as a woman with a disability, be respected in the federal government? Except for my eighteen months working in the Senate when I was twenty-five and my brief tenure in the California Department of Rehabilitation with Ed Roberts, I'd almost always been working alongside other disability activists, surrounded by people who also had disabilities. I still had a certain anxiety about being the only person in the room with a disability.

But my bigger issue was that I didn't want to leave where I was living. In California, I knew I could find people who could help me get up, go to the bathroom, and go to bed. I knew how to get around to see my friends. Jorge and I liked our life. In my job at WID, I had assistance in the office and there was no question about what I would do if there was a problem. We just helped each other out; we were like family.

In DC, in this new position, I would be responsible for four hundred staff, with a budget of about ten billion dollars under my management. I knew DC didn't have very many good disability-run organizations and it was hard to find personal assistants. And, if I was able to find one, I was concerned about logistics. In Berkeley, everyone could walk or ride their bikes to get where they needed to go, but in DC, people were often dependent on trains, which made me nervous. What if the trains weren't running on time and my personal assistant was late—and that made me late to a meeting or unable to meet a deadline? Or what if I wanted to get up at five in the morning to do my email or get ready for a meeting, how could someone get to my house that early if the trains weren't running until six?

I talked to Jorge about all my fears. I was also worried about him. Did he really want to move to DC? He had friends in Berkeley, and a job. This would have a big impact on him.

"Don't worry about me," he said. "You go for it. You're *chingona*."

In the end, I took the job

And, by the way, if you look up *chingona* at Urbandictionary .com, this is what you'll find: "Chingonas are the most badass girls in the world. Don't mess with them or they will kick you in the nalgas."

FOR A NUMBER of months before my appointment was confirmed by the Senate, I traveled to DC and worked as a consultant for two weeks a month. It allowed me to learn the job and attend meetings. I wasn't sitting in my office or making decisions, but was absorbing as much as I could before I assumed the position. I was up early and late, meeting tons of people, and traveling up a steep learning curve. It was like drinking from a fire hose, and, quite frankly, I loved it.

But do you know what is harder and more daunting than the prospect of managing four hundred staff and ten billion dollars under the eyes of a country made up of two hundred sixty three million people and a bicameral Congress?

Finding an accessible three-bedroom apartment and personal assistance in Washington, DC.

I had decided that the only way I could do the job would be if I had two people actually living with us, who could help me get up and go to bed, and work for me on the weekends. But three-bedroom apartments in DC were scarce, and finding an *accessible* three-bedroom was like shooting a rocket through a pinhole.

We looked at apartment buildings all over DC. Just when we were on the verge of giving up, we found one. Luckily, it was in a great neighborhood with two bus stops, two metro stations, a library, a grocery store, and some restaurants.

Now, personal assistance.

In the office, like the other assistant secretaries, I had an executive assistant and two other administrative people who helped me manage my schedule. The way we sorted out my personal assistance at work was by having the two people who helped me with administrative things also travel with me and help me with things like attending work-related functions and going to the bathroom. It was on the home front that I needed help. Anticipating problems finding people in DC, I'd already interviewed some people from California. I'd met a nice young woman named Andrea. She seemed like she could do the job so I checked her references, hired her, and gave her money to drive across the country. It seemed like we were finally going to have things sorted.

Anticipating her arrival, I waited. But she didn't show up.

Assuming there had just been some kind of mishap or delay on the trip across country, I somehow reached her and she told me she was in Georgia. She said she'd come the next day.

Again, she didn't show up.

I got the message. I just called her and said, "Forget it."

Eventually I did find two nice people. But the whole process made me anxious. Imagine. It's already anxiety provoking enough to have to interview and hire people to help you with some of the most intimate and essential activities in your life— and then to have them not show up!

Once we were installed in our apartment and set up, Jorge had to find a job. He'd given up his work in California so we could move, which he was happy to do for me, but in DC he faced a double-pronged challenge. He was disabled and he spoke English as a second language. And he was in Washington, which was much more conservative than the liberal bastion of Berkeley. It took him a long, long time to find a job.

This is how I became the highest-ranking disabled person in the US government.

I GOT to work.

OSERS had a reputation for being paternalistic and not listening to the people. Remember how I lied to Rehab in college about wanting to be a speech therapist when I really wanted to be a teacher? Because friends told me Rehab wouldn't let me be a teacher if there were no disabled people who were already teaching. And then Rehab tried to push me into being a social worker. That was Rehabilitation Services, which was now under my wing. So, first things first, I wanted to make damn sure that we gave disabled people a real voice in government, and my team needed to reflect that.

I wanted Howard Moses to be my deputy. Howard, who had cerebral palsy, was immensely talented and experienced. Although I hadn't worked with Howard before, he was well known and respected by people I trusted. I recommended him to the secretary and he was offered the job. Howard's knowledge about government and his personal and professional experience were critical to the work we did. One of the issues we immediately had to deal with was low morale among some of the staff. We wanted people to understand that we didn't just want their quality work but also their ideas. Howard, who became loved and deeply respected by the staff, made a big difference in this way.

Howard and I set about hiring our three top people. Fred Schroeder was confirmed to be the commissioner of the Rehabilitation Services Administration. Fred, who was blind, had a background in education and rehabilitation and was an active member of the National Federation of the Blind.

Katherine Seelman, who was deaf, became the director of the National Institute on Disability and Rehabilitation Research. Her focus was on science, technology, and public policy, especially telecommunications and accessibility. Kate also had a background working with people who had developmental disabilities.

Tom Hehir, who was director of Special Education Programs, didn't have a disability himself, but had a strong background working with poor minority and disabled students. Tom had deep experience and a real belief that all children could learn. This team was driven to make a difference.

OSERS had the most staff with disabilities of any office in the Department of Education, but when we arrived, we discovered that some staff didn't have the support they needed to effectively do their jobs. For instance, sign language interpreters were shared, and that limited people's ability to communicate. Some blind staff members also were not getting the support they needed. So we made some changes. We made sure some of our staff were assigned the responsibility of helping our blind employees read, when necessary, and we had sign language interpreters permanently on staff for our deaf employees. This was a big change from before, where deaf staff had to book interpreters for a specific meeting or event.

Because really? You're the director of the National Institute on Disability and Rehabilitation Services and have sixty staff, but you can only talk to them for the two hours you've booked a sign language interpreter three days ago? Or, you're in the elevator and run into an important member of Congress you've been trying to connect with for weeks about something, but, darn it, no sign language interpreter? Obviously, our deaf employees didn't need interpreters every single minute, but because interpreters are also people with more than just a singular talent for translating spoken language into sign language, they also contributed plenty of other valuable work.

One of the primary roles of OSERS is to implement the policies and laws that Congress passes, as well as support the development of relevant legislation by testifying, commenting, and drafting legislation.

Because I'd had my disability when I was young, I had a unique perspective on our work and a unique set of skills. I'd been a *recipient* of special ed and rehab, and I'd been a leader in the independent living movement. I knew global disability issues. The year and a half I'd spent in the Senate, although short, proved very important because I knew my way around congressional hearings and testimony and I knew of the staff and politicians. Although I probably didn't realize it fully before accepting the position at OSERS, it turned out to be the culmination of all these experiences that had prepared me.

Howard, Fred, Kate, Tom, and I had a vision and a single-minded focus: equality. In very simple terms, we wanted disabled kids to go to real schools with everyone else and we wanted disabled adults to have the opportunity to get hired for any job they were qualified for—and we were going to do everything we possibly could to make this happen. Frequently this put me on the front lines.

It was a stressful time. We were in the middle of the reauthorization of IDEA and the Republicans wanted to make changes relating to the expulsion from school of kids with emotional disabilities. We were saying that no child should be separated from education. We wanted to be sure that if a child had an emotional disability, they would receive the services they needed in the setting that was best for them, and expulsion served no purpose. Our position was that we had to find a way of giving them an education.

In the midst of the discussions, I got a call from the assistant secretary of legislative affairs.

"We need to get over to the White House," she said.

I rolled out the door immediately. Senior staff were discussing whether or not we could hew to our position of opposing expulsion of emotionally disabled children. I arrived just as the meeting was breaking up, but at the last minute was able to make our case. They ended up supporting our position.

Throughout my time in the Clinton administration, I constantly felt that the stakes were high, that lives depended on us.

Even though my own life experiences prepared me to be a different kind of leader than OSERS had probably ever had, I was still dealing with a sense of insecurity those experiences left in me. I often felt conflicted between wanting to be accepted but also knowing that I had to fight the status quo.

I was in an anteroom at my office, sitting on a couch, when my mother came in. I looked down at myself.

I was completely naked.

Suddenly I woke up. It was dark. Next to me I could hear Jorge breathing softly. I looked at the clock; it was three in the morning. It was a dream I had more than once.

OUR ROLE IN IMPLEMENTATION required that we ensure that the laws Congress passed were interpreted accurately and complied with. The federal government allocates funding for the education of disabled children to the state and local level based on certain laws, policies, programs, and grant opportunities. The actual spending decisions are then made by the individual states and cities, while following certain formulas and being monitored from the federal level. It was through this monitoring and grant-making process that we had influence over how things happened.

We made space for disabled people and parents to have a voice in how the money got spent at the local level. We improved teacher training so that educators were better trained in special education, diversity, and other important aspects of our services.

For the competitive grants, we were able to determine the criteria for the grants, consistent with congressional parameters. We had about a billion dollars to allocate, which in US government terms is not *that* much money—just to put it in perspective, the US was spending somewhere over $500 billion on education annually at that time—but still it is a great deal of money. I took that responsibility very seriously.

I worked hard to push down the doors, open the windows, and let people in. My goal was to share power. To listen. To collaborate. I'd roll the halls and drop in on staff, which sometimes drove people crazy, but anybody could come in and talk to me at any time.

I continued to serve for most of Bill Clinton's two terms in office, seven and a half years.

So, do I think we made a difference? I believe we did. People tell me that we changed the culture of OSERS, that we made the people we were serving matter and gave them a voice. But I guess only time will tell.

Change never happens at the pace we think it should. It happens over years of people joining together, strategizing, sharing, and pulling all the levers they possibly can. Gradually, excruciatingly slowly, things start to happen, and then suddenly, seemingly out of the blue, something will tip.

CHAPTER 11

HUMANS

THE VILLAGE WAS in a remote corner of Andhra Pradesh, where water came from wells and there was no electricity to be found. Sitting on a dusty path in my wheelchair I barely registered the heat and humidity, engrossed as I was in the discussion happening around me. Twenty disability activists from rural southeastern India were telling me about their lives.

"It was this boy," said a man who leaned into a pair of crutches, one leg visibly smaller than the other, and gestured to a little boy sitting at his mother's feet. Only about two years old, he was cute, with short curly hair, big brown eyes, and a bright smile on his face.

The man continued: "His mother came to us when he was just a newborn and asked for our help. 'My mother-in-law has told me not to feed my child,' she said. Because he had been born without arms, the grandmother did not want him to live."

"We went to the police," a woman in a wheelchair picked up the story, "and told them what the grandmother was doing. They came and talked to the grandmother and forced her to stop pressuring the mother. And now, you see, the boy is strong."

"How have things changed since you started organizing?" I asked the men and women, while the little child still played with his marker at his mother's feet.

"Well, they're now calling us by our names," said a different man, who was blind.

"They used to just call us by our disability—'limper,' 'blind,' 'deaf,'" said another.

In another village I sat on the porch of a small house. Cords ran out the windows, bringing electricity from the house next door. The village paths around us were dotted with wells. It was monsoon season and the heat pressed. This group of disability activists was full of mothers of children with very significant disabilities who were fighting to get the ID cards that would allow their children to go to school. They reminded me of the parents I had met all over my own country, fighting for their kids' education. And my friends' parents. They reminded me of my mother. Being in this village made me feel empowered.

The conditions were quite different from ours, but they cared about the same things. Autonomy and dignity and gaining access to fair laws.

On a later trip, to Uganda, I again found myself in a village with dusty dirt roads, no running water, and no electricity. In the center of the village, outside a small hut, I met with a group of people with disabilities. One person sat in a wheelchair, an old-fashioned wicker chair similar to the one used by Franklin D. Roosevelt some forty years earlier. Others were parents of young kids who appeared to have cerebral palsy, and there was an older blind woman. As was my custom, I started driving my motorized wheelchair around the circle to shake everyone's hand.

Suddenly a wail filled the air. Stunned, we all looked around to see what was wrong.

A boy about two years old was clinging to his mother's leg and staring at me, petrified. Hastily I drove my wheelchair to take my place in the circle. As soon as my chair moved, he began wailing and crying again. Unsure of myself, I stopped moving, embarrassed that the boy appeared to be afraid of me. As soon as I stopped moving, he stopped screaming. When I moved forward, he screamed again.

Then my interpreter leaned over and said, "I'm so sorry. He seems to be afraid of your chair." The child had never seen anyone in a motorized wheelchair.

I knew that a moving object, seeming to move by itself, could certainly be frightening. I'd experienced many adults and children who had never seen a motorized wheelchair, frequently staring. But the fear of this strange object that actually helps disabled persons was also a testament to the lack of support for disability and independence.

When I started at the World Bank, James Wolfensohn, an Australian with wide-ranging talents from fencing to playing the cello, was in charge. President Wolfensohn was in the process of reforming the institution in several ways, but one issue that had his laser focus was development for the poorest of the poor. Which was part of the reason I had been hired. The Adviser on Disability and Development's job was to get disability on the radar for the staff, to integrate a disability lens across the institution. This was complicated and challenging, not only because institutional change is hard, especially in organizations straddling multiple countries and cultures, but also because people all over the world, no matter where they work, have biases.

I'll give you an example. There was a time when President Wolfensohn was convening a group of youths from around the world. I got involved and investigated to find out whether any disabled youths had been invited. No, I discovered. Not one young person with a disability had been nominated to attend.

"Could we nominate someone?" I asked.

Because of the late notice, we had three or four short days to find a disabled youth to be nominated. At that time, I had two staff working under me. We got the word out through our network.

One of the names we got was Victor Pineda. "Victor is a very smart, very outgoing guy. He speaks seven languages and by the way, he uses a motorized wheelchair and a ventilator," someone wrote to us. We submitted Victor's name for the convening, along with several others.

Not too long after, one of my staff got a call from the office that was handling the event. On Victor's behalf, they were worried. They wanted to exclude him from the meeting, which was in France. What if there was a problem with his breathing machine in Paris? What would they do?

I told my staff I'd handle it. I called the person back.

"I am quite sure," I said, "that if someone has a medical problem in Paris the medical system in Paris will be able to handle it. And by the way, there might be other people in Paris who have medical problems."

I also sent an email, to be sure my response was documented.

Victor Pineda lives in Berkeley now, where he is a globally recognized scholar on development and urban design, as well as a filmmaker and the founder of Inclusive Cities Lab/World Enabled. He teaches at Berkeley. He has attended the Burning Man Festival and travels all over the world. He is the same very smart and very outgoing person I was first introduced to, but we would never have known what he could do if we had assumed that we knew his needs better than he knew them himself.

Of course, this is just one small example, and our work at the World Bank was much broader and encompassed the larger work that the World Bank was created to do, which was to make loans to countries for major projects—but it does show the type of well-meaning assumptions people unconsciously make all the time, in many small but damaging ways. In response, we offered staff across the institution a multitude of opportunities to understand and learn about disability and what it meant on a day-to-day basis for us.

It was at the World Bank that I ran into my biggest experience of bullying. I had a superior who was a nondisabled man. He was constantly micromanaging and nitpicking my work, right up until I decided to leave in 2007, four years later. Was he bullying me in particular? It is true that he was written up for bullying other women who were not disabled—but my biggest issue was with myself. When my superior said and did outrageous things to me I cowered inside. Being in a segregated environment for so long had been good and bad for me—good because it gave me space to grow my confidence, but bad because I didn't learn how to be a part of the nondisability community in a forthright way. Bullies often choose people they perceive as the most isolated and marginalized—and the stereotype of disabled people fits that description, which makes us a target. Because of the segregated environment I'd grown up in, I didn't have a lot of experience with nondisabled men, which made it even harder. In response, I didn't do things that I felt a man in my position would have done; for example, I never went over my superior's head. I did speak with the ombudsman about the bullying, but that went nowhere. I was conflicted internally about how to deal with it. In the end I stopped trying to do anything, worried that I would become branded as unemployable, and, unfortunately, the reality was that nothing was likely to happen anyway.

I was a big fan of James Wolfensohn, though. He and I met regularly. When he left the bank, I soon left too.

Not long after the World Bank work, I took a position with the District of Columbia, where I was responsible for the Developmental Disability Administration and the Rehabilitation

Services Administration. I had been with the District for about three years and was sitting in my office at the intersection of Fifteenth and K Streets when I got a call from the State Department.

It was the State Department staff member in charge of political appointments.

"Would you be interested in being interviewed for a position that has just been created?" I was immediately excited. I knew exactly what position she was talking about.

"Yes," I said to the woman from the State Department. "I'm interested."

After an historic election for the country eight months earlier, Barack Obama had assumed office. He was charismatic and well spoken, confident and a leader. He had a vision for moving us out of the recession, and the minority communities clearly wanted to give him a chance. Just a month before he had signed the United Nations Convention on the Rights for People with Disabilities (CRPD). It was huge.

The CRPD is an international human rights treaty intended to protect the rights and dignity of persons with disabilities. Countries that sign and ratify the treaty are required to promote, protect, and ensure the human rights of people with disabilities and ensure that they enjoy full equality under the law. At that time, and still today, the convention served as a major catalyst in the global movement for changing how disabled people are seen—that is, no longer as objects of charity, medical treatment, and social protection but rather as full and equal members of society, with human rights.

While at the World Bank I had attended a number of the meetings convened at the UN headquarters in New York to develop the CRPD. In many ways the treaty was modeled on legislation like the Americans with Disabilities Act. For that reason the Bush administration had said it would not sign or ratify it—because the US didn't need it. Although the United States had an official delegation that attended all of the formal and drafting sessions, for many years delegation members were not allowed to formally engage with international colleagues.

And then President Obama was elected.

I had attended the ceremony at the White House where he and Secretary of State Hillary Clinton had announced that the US would sign the CRPD and would be creating a new position at the State Department to work toward the US ratifying the treaty. The Special Adviser on International Disability Rights would lead the effort to try to mobilize support for the CRPD in the Senate. If the Senate voted to approve the treaty, then Obama could ratify it. This special adviser would also be responsible for integrating a disability lens across the State Department. It was a role similar to the position I'd held at the World Bank, and it combined many things that I cared about. Plus, I knew Hillary Clinton from when we were both members of the American delegation to the World Conference on Women in Beijing in 1995, when she was First Lady, and I liked her.

A week after the phone call, I went to the interview. It was with the woman who had called me, and it must have gone fairly well because I was invited for a second interview. This time I met with Cheryl Mills, Hillary Clinton's chief of staff, who was also in charge of presidential affairs. A few weeks later they recommended me for the position, a political appointment by President Obama. I was very happy.

I called Jorge.

"They are recommending me for the position at the State Department," I told him.

"I told you," he said. "*Eres chingona.*" I could see the smile on his face through the phone.

Then the paperwork started. To get a security clearance I had to document all of my overseas travel for the past seven years. All the people I had met. Everything I'd done. It took nearly six months. When I finally received clearance, I was able to start. I reported to the assistant secretary of democracy, human rights, and labor. I was thrilled that they also accepted my recommendation to offer a political appointment to Kathy Guernsey, who I had worked with at the World Bank. We had a monumental task in front of us. Our job was to drive home the message that disability needed to be a part of the State Department's agenda. Foreign aid. Foreign service. Human rights. All of it.

It was June 2010, and I was sixty-three years old.

My first trip was to Tunisia, Algeria, and Jordan. The staff in our embassies there were interested in elevating the issue of disability and invited us to visit. We got to work planning the trip.

The very first thing I wanted to figure out was how to make disabled people visible. As long as we were out of sight, we were out of mind, which made us not only easier to discount but easier to hurt, and worse.

Our base for the first leg of the trip was the US embassy in Tunis. The ambassador agreed to hold a dinner and invited a group of disabled activists and people who were working on advancing the rights of disabled people. We also planned a series of meetings leading up to and following the dinner. I wanted to learn about the major issues disabled people were addressing and for the disabled activists to come into the embassy and meet our ambassador and staff face-to-face. Our people needed to hear directly from people with disabilities about the types of human rights violations that were happening in Tunisia. We worked with the State Department staff on the ground in Tunisia to organize all the logistics of the trip.

Right away it became apparent that the work of simply organizing the logistics of our trip and dinner was going to serve a purpose in and of itself. My status as a disabled person in a senior position raised the issue to a higher level than would otherwise have been the case. We had to get on the phone and talk with the staff to help them think through every single detail of accessibility. Everything had to be accessible, from the offices where we had meetings to the restaurants and hotels to the embassy entrance and rooms to providing sign language interpretation to providing Braille printed materials. And of course many things were not accessible. Even the embassy itself wasn't quite accessible enough. The ADA has limited reach abroad. New embassies and renovations were complying with federal standards around construction but, as I was to learn, with most of the embassies it was hit or miss for accessibility.

Interestingly, doing the work to plan our trip turned out to be a learning exercise not only for the team in our embassies but sometimes also for the people with whom we met. In Jordan we had a meeting with the mayor of Amman. To deal with getting into the city hall, which wasn't accessible, we borrowed some portable ramps from the World Bank. We'd mentioned to some of the key people on the Jordan side, "You should think about what it would take to make your city hall accessible."

"We'll do it," was the response we got, "but it will take a year."

While we were in the meeting with the mayor, however, we told him about this conversation and he walked down to look at the entrance.

Two weeks later the city hall in Amman had a wheelchair ramp, designed in the architectural style of the building. It was a truly refreshing response.

Lack of exposure and lack of knowledge. These were the two biggest problems we faced with people. Not that unusual.

When we came back from the Middle East, we organized a screening for State Department staff of *Lives Worth Living*, a documentary about the US disability rights movement. It told the story of everything we'd done, from just after World War II to passage of the ADA. It was our first big event. We invited a panel of experts from the World Bank, Human Rights Watch, and other organizations, and held the event in a big conference room. Over a hundred people came. Afterward a friend who was a director at the one of the regional offices for the State Department approached me.

"Until I saw this film," she said, "I didn't understand that there was a civil rights movement for disabled people."

I was flummoxed.

It had been twenty years since the ADA had passed and thirty-five since Section 504 had been signed—a whole generation ago. And this was a person who worked in human rights every day, someone who was knowledgeable about the world. Yet it was the first time she'd either heard, or really understood, that Section 504 and the ADA was about our civil and human rights. And she was not the only one to tell me this.

The problem was that the ADA had been passed without the same level of consciousness-raising experienced around African Americans and the civil rights movement. Consequently, disability rights activists continued to be at a serious disadvantage.

We showed *Lives Worth Living* several times throughout my time at the State Department, and I continued to hear the same thing from many, many people. Like at the World Bank, like people all over the world, people have limited awareness of the problems and the solutions.

At the State Department we had a program called the Mandela Fellows, which was a prestigious program for young Africans. People were selected to come to the US, where they had the opportunity to go to a university for six weeks and learn about human rights–related issues; then they'd come to DC for a few days; and then some of them would go to work for an organization for a month. At one point people in my department were submitting names of people, nominating them to be a part of this program. As the application deadline loomed, naturally I asked if any disabled youths were being nominated. Nobody knew. So we jumped into action. We reached out to the organizations working on disability issues in Africa to ask them to nominate some disabled young people.

One of the people we heard about was a young man who was getting his master's at American University in Washington. We nominated him and he was accepted.

Then someone from the program called us. Now you know how this story goes. This person was worried about how, given his disability, the young man would get to the required meetings at the White House and the State Department. I winced when I heard this.

"Call the Mandela Fellows program back," I said to my staff person, "and tell them this: He got from Uganda to American University. We're quite sure he can get from American University to the State Department and the White House."

A certain unconscious, unspoken logic continued to operate.

In a meeting about education for children with disabilities, someone said to me, "Let's just deal with education for non-disabled children first. Then we can worry about the kids with disabilities."

It was all very familiar. The basic logic goes something like this: People with disabilities won't benefit as much from x, or y, or z, as people without disabilities, which means, therefore, that x, or y, or z, is not essential. They should accept the idea of going without. The same goes for other issues, like transportation and employment.

But what kind of logic is this?

The underlying assumption is that people with disabilities have less potential to learn, less ability to contribute, are less capable. That we are less equal. Do we really believe this?

Disability is a natural aspect of the human condition. As people live longer, as we fight more wars, as medical care continues to improve—more and more people who might have died in an earlier era will live. Perhaps with a disability. We should accept it. Plan for it. Build our society around it.

At the State Department, gradually people began to understand what we were talking about. At the embassy level, where they made most of the nominations for participants in State Department programs, the staff started to get a better understanding of what we meant. Namely, when you're looking for youths, look for disabled youths, male and female—and not only the people with the mildest disabilities. In some cases, someone would need a personal assistant, and State would pay for the assistant, too, who also got approval for their visa. Or if the person needed a different sort of accommodation, that became more possible than it had been in the past.

By the time I left the State Department, there were sixty-five disabled Mandela fellows, whereas when we first started there were none. Many of these fellows have gone on to become leaders in their countries. Furthermore, none of the fellows had been getting sent for their work experience to disability organizations, so we added disability organizations to the list of places where people could go on their fellowship. The Center for Independent Living of the Hudson Valley was looking at issues about violence against women with disabilities, and a fellow went there for his work session.

You drop a petal in the water and it has a ripple effect.

The good thing was, most people were open and they were learning. As they learned, they started to get a better understanding of what we were really trying to do.

Have you ever noticed how some words are just words—until you really see or hear how something feels?

Like hatred.

Or discrimination.

Or human rights.

We underappreciate our human rights in America. But human rights are like salamanders: you don't notice they're disappearing until suddenly you realize they've gone. In Nazi Germany, as my father would write many years after the fact, no one in his village noticed what was happening until it was too late.

To try to get the Senate to approve the CRPD, we were having regular meetings and conversations at the State Department with officials from the Department of Justice, the Department of Health and Human Services, and the Bureau of Legislative Affairs. A detailed analysis was being done on the compatibility of the requirements of the CRPD with the current legislation on the books in the US. There were multiple hearings on the treaty. Most of this work was being done in the trenches among the officials and staff representatives from the various departments. Although Hillary Clinton was well versed in what was going on, other priorities meant she wasn't deep in it day to day.

When John Kerry came in as secretary of state in February 2013, he was much more hands-on with CRPD than Hillary.

We had much more interaction with Secretary Kerry than I had with Hillary. He chaired some of the meetings of civil society groups invited in to hear about what we were doing, and he testified at a hearing. I was often part of a team briefing him on relevant issues. He had been on the Senate Foreign Affairs Committee and was well versed in international issues.

Simultaneously, the disability community was working on it as well—the US Council on Disability was trying to educate people about why the convention was important. Jon Wodatch, a former employee of the Department of Justice, helped, and many, many disabled people's organizations mobilized in support of it. Eventually, CRPD got passed by its committee.

But there were also people fighting ratification of the convention. Rumors and myths were developing and getting passed around. People said the CRPD would allow the UN to come in and take children away from their families. One group organized a thousand people to call their senators and jam their home lines. In the end, in spite of all our work, CRPD went down. In the twenty-plus years since the Republicans and Democrats had collaborated to pass the ADA in 1990, things had changed. People were more concerned about using their power to score political points against each other than in working out a way to do the arduous work necessary to compromise and reach consensus. Although a small number of Republicans did support it, we couldn't get enough.

The US generally does not like to ratify UN treaties. We often think we can go it alone instead. But whether or not we can go it alone is not really the right question. The better question is, who do we want to be? I know we're a nation that cares about the most vulnerable and marginalized people. What side of history do we want to be on?

You might be wondering, What has happened with the ADA? Especially since the year 2015 marked a quarter of a century since the ADA was passed?

Passage of the ADA has meant that curb cuts and ramps are now routinely created to facilitate wheelchair use, and access to education, transport, and jobs has cracked open. More awareness and expertise on the part of the disability activists has emerged.

Businesses unwilling to comply have been taken to court, and cases have been won and lost, setting precedents and, with them, creating expectations. Backlash has also come.

In response, in 2008, Congress, under President George W. Bush, passed the ADA Amendments Act in an effort to protect and restore the intention of the original act.

Then, just months after President Obama's twenty-fifth-anniversary celebration of the ADA, in 2015, held in the East Room of the White House, the ADA Education and Reform Act was introduced to weaken enforcement of the regulations. The act shows the extent to which some legislators are willing to allow for excuses to be made for lack of compliance.

President Obama protected the ADA. His administration had a very strong domestic agenda for people with disabilities. In particular, he targeted our next frontiers. Curb cuts and ramps are essential, but if you put in a ramp and nothing else happens, then no one will go up the ramp.

Obama hired people with disabilities to work in the White House and appointed people with disabilities throughout the government. He hired people with knowledge and vision, and focused on education and employment for disabled people. Although much progress had been made, significantly lower numbers of us were going to college than were nondisabled peers, we were also much more likely to be unemployed, and we were much more likely to live in poverty than nondisabled people.

Obama recommended increased funding for IDEA, the educational act for children with disabilities that I had worked on. He recommitted the US government to hiring one hundred thousand people with disabilities, convened gatherings with the leading designers of autonomous vehicles and disabled people to ensure disability would be taken into account in their development, and did a number of other important things in this vein.

But the biggest thing he did was to get the Affordable Care Act, known as Obamacare, passed. The Affordable Care Act allowed disabled people, who were getting denied health insurance because of preexisting conditions, to get insurance; it also made health insurance more affordable; and expanded Medicaid, a federal program that covered healthcare for children and those who are low income, elderly, or disabled.

CHAPTER 12

OUR STORY

SOMETIMES HOLLYWOOD TRIES to tell our story. You've seen the movie.

A woman acquires a disability, and wants to die, and then convinces a loved one to kill her. *Million Dollar Baby*.

A man acquires a disability, wants to die, but then falls in love with his personal attendant. To "save" her from a lifetime with a disabled man he kills himself. *Me Before You*.

A man acquires a disability and turns villainous in the face of the agony. *Star Wars'* Darth Vader.

Disability is seen as a burden, a tragedy.

But what if it wasn't?

What if someone's story began with the words: "I never wished I didn't have a disability."

Even today, it is difficult for me to remember how I felt the night before my mother took me to register for kindergarten. How carefully I picked my dress and laid it out for my first day of school. How painful it was to feel rejected.

In my own mind, there were no barriers to what I could learn or what I could achieve. All the barriers came from outside of me.

Has having a disability made me different than I would have been? Of course I don't know the answer to that question. Would you be different if you'd been born Buddhist or Muslim—or grown up in Dakar instead of London? How do you know?

What I do know is that I've had to learn to push through my insecurities.

I've learned I'm stronger in a group.

I know having my disability has given me opportunities I wouldn't have had if I hadn't had it. If I'd simply been a girl growing up in Brooklyn, I wouldn't have been exposed to the same things.

I know it pushed me to study harder, work harder, and achieve harder. To travel.

I know it pushed me to fight. To change how others saw us— our human potential.

Would I have met Ed and Frieda, Joni and Mary Lou, Pat and Kitty, CeCe and Kalle, Adolf, Eunice, and Diane?

Would I have been open to Jorge?

My life would have been totally different. And the same.

How can anyone know what their life would have been?

I can only know that it was meant to be what it is. I am who I was meant to be.

If you were to acquire a disability tomorrow it would be a change. But I can tell you this: it wouldn't have to be a tragedy.

We are all human. Why do we see disability differently from any other aspect of being human?

When I look back now, I see that one of the greatest aspects of the 504 sit-in was the way it united us. We weren't focused on how we were different—we were focused on our common goal, our collective purpose. We looked beyond how we each spoke and moved, how we thought and how we looked. We respected the humanity in each other.

We stood for inclusiveness and community, for our love of equity and justice—and we won.

ON AN UNUSUALLY warm day in January 2017, Jorge and I were
watching television in our apartment in Washington.

A transfer of power was taking place for the forty-fifth time
in US history. President-elect Donald Trump was getting sworn
in. As he began to speak, rain started to fall outside the Capitol
Building. His speech was just under twenty minutes long and it
hit my heart like a torpedo.

"From this day forward, a new vision will govern," he said.
"It's going to be only America first." I recognized that phrase. It
had its roots in white nationalism and nativism.

In the brief period of time he spoke, President Trump's lack
of respect for others came clearly through.

"What have we done?" I said to Jorge, the hairs on the back of
my neck standing on end.

But the truth is, Donald Trump spoke like any other political
leader who wants to take advantage of distance and segregation,
of inequality.

Equally, we have leaders who stand for the opposite. And we
have ourselves.

The day after Trump's inauguration, women filled the streets.
These women were also outraged by President Trump's lack of
respect. They were protesting his litany of negative statements
about women. Wearing pink hats with cat ears, a reference to
Trump's casual remark about grabbing women by the pussy,
women from all over the world marched—in DC, Hong Kong,
and Paris; in Buenos Aires and London. The 2017 Women's
March would exceed all previous numbers in US history for a
single-day protest. Multiple marches around the world would
draw millions of people.

We have come a long way from my youth. The legislation we
worked so hard to get passed still stands: the Americans with
Disabilities Act, Section 504, IDEA, and numerous other federal

and state laws validate and protect the civil rights of people with disabilities. Disabled children are no longer allowed to be denied the right to an education. Calling a child a fire hazard is illegal. Representatives of the American Public Transit Association speak at international meetings, advocating for accessible transportation. As of today, a hundred and seventy-seven countries and counting have ratified the UN Convention on the Rights of Persons with Disabilities. And someday, hopefully, we too will ratify.

If you're of an age where you've grown up with all these benefits—curb cuts, disabled kids in class, captioning and audio description on television, and the myriad other ways disabled people are integrated into our communities—you would be forgiven for thinking that this is how it is, how it's always been, and how it always will be. It would be understandable if you took these rights for granted.

But our government is constantly changing. It was created by groups of people and it gets changed by groups of people.

This presents us with a choice:

Do we want to be the people creating the government we believe in, or do we want to be the people simply accepting whatever comes our way?

During his campaign, Donald Trump mocked a reporter with a disability.

After assuming the presidency, he did much more. Donald Trump immediately made many changes affecting disability issues. From day one, he went after the Affordable Care Act. On his first day in office, he signed an executive order that actually directed federal agencies to reduce the enforcement of requirements related to the act. A decisive first step toward repealing the law.

He appointed a secretary of education, Betsy DeVos, unfamiliar with the Individuals with Disabilities Education Act.

He shut down the ADA pages on the White House website.

He signed an executive order for federal departments "to alleviate unnecessary regulatory burdens."

Donald Trump's actions are good examples of how attacks on civil rights can happen. These kinds of attacks don't always come through the front door; often they slide stealthily through any crack they can find. Shutting down the ADA pages on the White House website, ordering staff "to alleviate unnecessary regulatory burdens," hiring senior staff who neither know the legislation they are mandated to enforce nor believe in what the law requires, or not hiring staff at all are stealthy, slippery snakes looking for the cracks in the civil rights laws.

Under the management of DeVos, seventy-two policy guidelines that interpreted and explained the rights of students with disabilities under IDEA disappeared from the government website. It is guidelines like these, documents that clarify and explain laws and policies, that can make the difference in people's ability to know and advocate for their rights. If someone violates your civil rights, your main recourse involves making a complaint. But if you don't know or you don't fully understand the laws and regulations, how do you know to make a complaint? It's a slippery slope. When laws and policies get less visible, it becomes more and more difficult to know whether an action is even considered a violation of your civil rights.

In response to the Trump administration's attacks, the disability activist community kicked into high gear in multiple ways, organizing protests, raising awareness, educating people.

Six months after Jorge and I watched Donald Trump's inauguration, people with disabilities were lying sprawled on the floor outside Senate Majority Leader Mitch McConnell's office. It was a die-in, organized by ADAPT. In a full-blown attempt to repeal Obama's Affordable Care Act, the Senate had developed an alternative healthcare plan, and it included deep cuts to Medicaid. Without the medical care and services funded by Medicaid, ten million disabled people faced the real possibility of having to live in institutions. This "die-in" was just one of the protests the disability activists had organized to fight the proposed changes.

Reporters covered the die-in for television news programs. Security guards forcibly removed the protesters from their wheelchairs and carried them out, reminding me of the day we got kicked by the guards in front of Joseph Califano's office.

In the end, the attempt to repeal Obamacare was defeated. Due, in no small part, to the efforts of the activists.

When protecting civil rights, however, activism is only half the equation. The other half involves the justice system.

President Trump's first attorney general was a longtime senator named Jeff Sessions. As a senator Jeff Sessions had attacked IDEA, the education law I worked on that supports education for kids with disabilities.

IDEA is the "single most irritating problem for teachers throughout America today," Sessions said, calling it "a complex system of federal regulations and laws that have created lawsuit after lawsuit, special treatment for certain children, and that are a big factor in accelerating the decline in civility and discipline in classrooms all over America."[1] He went on to read several letters from a group of Alabama educators and principals, all complaining about discipline issues, which they blamed on disabled students and the IDEA.

Not only is it outrageous to blame the needs of disabled children for the problems of the American school system, but also Sessions was clearly implying that the education of children with disabilities was not of equal priority with the education of other children.

In other words, he didn't support the law of the country. And this is the leader whom President Trump had selected to be the country's highest-ranking legal official, responsible for enforcing the law.

Two and a half years into the Trump administration, the president had nominated over a hundred judges to the federal courts—nominees who, according to the *Guardian*, "have records of working tirelessly to undermine access to healthcare, access to reproductive rights for women, who want to undermine critical protections for workers, for clean air and clean water that consumers rely on. . . . The people who are going to suffer are the millions of people around the country who rely on these critical, essential legal rights and protections that for the next three or four decades are going to be seriously eroded."[2]

Our courts and our judges matter. Our system of justice matters. Civil rights laws are meaningful when people understand the law, advocate for themselves and others, *and* can rely on the justice system to effectively monitor and enforce the law.

What if I hadn't gotten Constance Baker Motley as my judge, and the courts had upheld the actions of a doctor who asked me to show her how I went to the bathroom? What if she had agreed with a Board of Education that told me I couldn't be a teacher because I couldn't walk? My entire life would have gone very differently.

HOW DO WE move forward now?

It is true that people with disabilities continue to face challenges. Disabled people are twice as likely to be unemployed as nondisabled people. There's no dependable financial source for the personal assistance we need to be able to live independently. We're still stigmatized and regularly encounter discrimination and people assuming we're less qualified or are going to be burdensome in some way.

To confront these issues and move forward we must ask: What is our vision for our society?

Do we want our communities to be the types of neighborhoods and cities where our loved ones can choose to stay in their communities as they age? Where, if an accident happened to us or one of our children, we would be able to continue living in our community, going to our same school or working our same job?

We need to accept our humanity and design our world around it: use universal design; support personal assistance; change how we hire.

We *can* design our cities and our society in a way that fosters belonging and community, rather than segregation and isolation.

We can move from thinking it can't happen to saying it can happen, from being naysayers to being problem solvers.

Like kids.

Larger questions loom in my mind.

How we treat disabled people, how we treat minorities, boils down to our fundamental beliefs about humanity. Do we believe that we all have something to contribute, regardless of where we're from, how we move or think, the language we speak, the color of our skin, the religion we choose, and the people we love?

Do we believe in equality?

We need to look inside and think deeply about whether we really believe this to be true.

Because we already have the vehicle we need to make our society fair, to give everyone a voice, to protect and advance the rights of those who are marginalized, and create the shared institutions that support us all. It's our democracy.

If we keep valuing our democratic government and continue to invest in it, then we can solve problems of inequality. But we have to resist the temptation to give up on it when it gets complicated, because democracy is complex and its processes necessarily take time. By its very nature it must be so.

Including everyone's voice, ensuring the protection of the marginalized, representing the diversity of our country—all this requires a democracy to look deeply into issues, have multiple discussions and committee meetings, and follow the types of checks and balances that take time. Decision-making takes time. Above all, we want a government that is able to examine the facts, be reasonably objective, and make people feel they're being heard.

If this isn't happening in the way we think it should, we can't give up on it. If it feels awkward and frustrating, we need to do something about it.

Perhaps we need to remember what Shirley Chisholm, the first black congresswoman and the author of *Unbossed and Unbought*, said: "You don't make progress by standing on the sidelines, whimpering and complaining. You make progress by implementing ideas."

She may have been scolding us, but she may also have been absolutely right. We can make it better.

Run for office.

Participate in elections.

"Vote, like your life depends on it, because it does!" as Justin Dart said.

Fight against the powers pushing to disenfranchise minorities, including those who have disabilities.

Become an activist.

We tend to stereotype activists, sometimes even making fun of them for their committees, their meetings, their multiple stakeholders. But this belies the strategy behind what we do.

The Section 504 sit-in was an exceedingly complex operation. First, it took years to develop the enabling regulations and create the American Coalition of Citizens with Disabilities, the national umbrella coordinating organization. Then it took many months and a multitude of meetings to organize the protest outside the San Francisco Federal Building. Our work was grounded in an enormous amount of networking among the civil rights groups, involving more people than you can imagine. Behind each name I've mentioned in this book were thousands of others, radiating outward. We had committee after committee after committee. Everyone had a role and everyone had ownership.

Why?

Because we believed that every single person had a role in producing the change. We knew our success would hinge on collaboration. Our power would only come from the people who identified with and felt ownership of a movement.

This is still how I operate today.

We—all of us, and especially marginalized people—need to work together. In the broader civil rights movements disability was and still is absent. Visible and invisible disabilities cut across all minorities. We are African American, Latino, Asian, Native American, gay, straight, transgender, middle class, wealthy, poor, Jewish, Hindu, Christian, Muslim. We can't be selective about which marginalized group moves forward. At the end of the day, we all need to be moving forward together, taking care of our families and the planet.

When whole groups of people become segregated from others in our society, it weakens the fabric of our democracy. Distance and segregation are breeding grounds for failures of understanding and empathy and ultimately injustice and the denial of others' rights. If we allow ourselves slowly to become a country where we are simply unable to imagine ourselves in another's shoes, we can't understand the complexity of how discrimination occurs and how it feels. Lacking respect for those we don't know or understand makes it easy to blame inequality and poverty on individuals—rather than on the system. Once we're caught up in blaming each other, how can we possibly create a society that values equality?

Sometimes it takes a long time for people to come forward. We have to move from passivity—from feeling like we're a lone, individual voice—to speaking actively, collectively. When I finally started school and went to camp for the first time, I met all these disabled people who had been experiencing the same things as me—after we'd all been feeling so alone. Why, we wondered, were we being excluded from society? How could we ever begin to achieve the American dream when we were not being given the same opportunities as others? Coming together, we were able to begin to articulate not only what was wrong, but what we thought was possible.

When we were united, it was as if progress happened overnight.

It gave us courage. Conviction. Strength.

Yes, we might be angry. We may not like some things our government does. We may worry.

But we have to remember that we have the power. We are changing things.

As Congresswoman Barbara Jordan said, "A government is invigorated when each of us is willing to participate in shaping the future of this nation."

For we are our leaders of inclusiveness and community, of love, equity, and justice.

ACKNOWLEDGMENTS

FROM JUDY AND KRISTEN

We would like, first and foremost, to thank all of the amazing activists and supporters whose stories loom large in this book. Some of you are no longer with us, but we have felt your influence no less strongly. Anita Aaron, Jan Balter, Gerald Baptiste, Joyce Bender, Frank Bowe, Mary Lou Breslin, Joni Breves, Marca Bristo, Kelly Buckland, Phil Burton, Jane Campbell, Theodore Childs, Bill Clinton, Hillary Clinton, Ann Cody, Tony Coelho, Rebecca Cokely, Kitty Cone, Alan Cranston, Annie Cupolo, Nancy D'Angelo, Denise Darensbourg, Justin and Yoshiko Dart, Eric Dibner, Phil Draper, Barbara Duncan, Edward Dwyer, Nik Edes, Fred Fay, Denise and Patricio Figueroa, Eunice Fiorito, Lex Freiden, HolLynn D'Lil Fuller, Bob Funk, Claudia Gordon, Kathy Guernsey, Tom Harkin, Tom Hehir, Susan Henderson, Ralf Hotchkiss, Rachel Hurst, Margaret "Dusty" Irvine, Joyce Jackson, Neil and Denise Jacobson, Deborah Kaplan, Ted Kennedy, John Kerry, Kalle Konkkola, John Lancaster, Julie Landau, Jim LeBrecht, Joan Leon, Mary Lester, Bobbi Linn, Diane Lipton, Brad Lomax, Doug Martin, Arlene Mayerson, Steve McClelland, Dennis McQuade, George Miller, Beatrice Mitchell, Howard Moses, Jeff Moyer, Ari Ne'eman, Barack Obama, Mary Jane Owen, Major Owens, Martin Paley, Karen Parker, Evelyn Protano, Joe Quinn, Adolf Ratzka,

Laura Rauscher, Joletta Reynolds, Curtis Richards, Richard Riley, Ed Roberts, Ann Rosewater, Katherine Salinas, Greg Sanders, Fred Schroeder, Kate Seelman, Joe Shapiro, Sigi Shapiro, Bobby Silverstein, Debbie Stanley, Max and Colleen Starkloff, Gloria Steinem, Susan Sygall, Frieda Tankas, Lynette Taylor, Maria Town, Ray Uzeta, Lisa Walker, Stephanie Walker, Ron Washington, CeCe Weeks, the Reverend Cecil Williams, Harrison Williams, Michael Winter, John Wodatch, Pat Wright, Ray Zanella, Theda Zawaiza, Hale Zukas, and too many more to name here.

We especially thank those of you who read multiple versions of this manuscript and provided invaluable feedback and commentary, particularly John Wodatch and Joan Leon, as well as Gabrielle George, Nicole Newnham, Robin Murray, Denise Figueroa, and Bette McMuldren. Susan Wardell of Otago University in New Zealand gave extremely comprehensive and helpful notes—also Catherine Main, Katy Smith, Lara Greenway, and Kelly Taylor. We are indebted to HolLynn D'Lil and her book *Becoming Real in 24 Days: One Participant's Story of the 1977 Section 504 Demonstrations for U.S. Civil Rights*, and to the University of California at Berkeley's Bancroft Library Oral History Project for their incredible foresight to interview the activists of the disability rights movement; both provided an invaluable record of events around the Section 504 sit-in.

This project would never have come to fruition without the spark provided by Jon Miller and Stuart James, who convinced Judy that she had a story that needed to be told and played matchmaker with us. Jill Marr, our agent at Sandra Dijkstra Literary Agency, and Kevin Cleary and John Beach of Gravity Squared Entertainment carried the project forward, cheered us on, and made us believe we could actually finish the book. Joanna Green, our editor, gave excellent editorial feedback, and the entire team at Beacon has been wonderful.

Finally, we are grateful for the opportunity we have had to learn from each other and work together. On Judy's part, it was a leap of faith to believe that Kristen, a nondisabled person, could understand her perspective and, on a more mundane level, that this book could be written across a great distance. On Kristen's part, she grew as a feminist and activist who was ashamed to find she had only a dim understanding of the disability rights movement to a true ally. We have enormous gratitude for the journey we took together—and we especially treasure all the time we spent conversing, debating, and arguing.

FROM JUDY

I want to thank my husband, Jorge Pineda, for his ongoing support of me and my work. When I met him in Eugene, Oregon, in 1991, our worlds were forever changed. Our values are aligned in our love of family and our fight for equality. Jorge left his country to join me in mine and this is something I will always appreciate. I have learned so much from him. He has given me a love of music and delicious food, and an understanding of the discrimination against Latinos, which continues despite their enormous contribution to the fabric of our country. We have traveled to Mexico, eaten many wonderful meals with his family, and spent time in amazing museums. I have been privileged with a close relationship with our nieces and nephews as they have grown up and visited us over the years. Recently we were talking about why we love each other and he told me that I was a wonderful woman and an activist. This being said, I know that making enough time for each other is always a challenge, I'm sure he rues the day he ever got me my first smart device in the 1990s.

I would like to thank my friends who have supported and encouraged me over the years to tell my story. My story is similar to so many other people's—those with and without disabilities. Telling our stories helps strengthen our ability to continue to fight against injustice. Sharing the stories about how we want our world to be—and then turning these dreams and visions into reality—is what we must all commit to doing.

I want to thank my mother and father, Ilse and Werner Heumann, for never giving up, and continuing to fight, both with me and for me. My mother, for her relentlessness and for being a role model who taught me in her own quiet and persistent way to fight for justice, not only in the area of disability but also to fight racial injustice. She taught me the importance of a diverse coalition. My father, for his belief in me and support of what my mother did, for all the meetings he drove us to and protests he and my mother attended, and for the number of times he drove me to my singing lessons with Dr. Dwyer.

My brothers, Joseph and Ricky, also helped me to become the person I am today.

FROM KRISTEN

I am tremendously grateful to my parents. My mother, Laurie Warnick Joiner, whom I miss dearly every day, taught me the art of writing while cooking dinner after a full day of work and to always question the status quo, and my father, Brian Joiner, taught me think critically. I so appreciate his Southern storytelling roots and my grandmother and great-aunts for their ability to make a walk to the store hilarious. I am grateful to my stepmother, Lynnie Clemons, for her amazing warmth and excellent comments. Pat and Cath Sandbrook, my in-laws, who gave loving support. My brother David was always willing to take a break from work to give advice and feedback. And my brother Kevin, who has been a big influence on me. I am grateful to Bill Murphy, executive director of Purpose Capital, who was extremely generous about giving me flexibility at work.

I couldn't have done this without my soul sisters, all of whom I wish I could name here. My best friend, Lucinda Treat, convinced me I could do this project, read everything, and is always relentlessly willing to listen. Jennifer McIver and Margot Szamier kept me sane.

To my beautiful family, I thank you again and again. Julian, Oliver, and Olivia, you tolerated long early-morning Skype sessions in the kitchen, sat in my lap to help copyedit (Olivia), made smart storytelling suggestions (Oliver), engaged in lengthy discussions about discrimination (Julian), and, most of all, kept me laughing. And Jon Sandbrook, my husband, you gently snow-plowed a path for me in our lives to make space for this. Thank you for refusing to allow me to do any housework for months, creating the coin-toss road trip to give me quiet time in the house during school holidays, and waking up with me at five to read drafts. I'd be lost without you.

NOTES

CHAPTER 6: OCCUPATION ARMY

1. HolLynn D'Lil, *Becoming Real in 24 Days: One Participant's Story of the 1977 Section 504 Demonstrations for U.S. Civil Rights* (N.P.: Hallevaland Productions, 2015), 130. My account of events of the sit-in draws on the detailed account provided in *Becoming Real in 24 Days*. See especially 112–15.

CHAPTER 7: SOLDIERS IN COMBAT

1. Andrew Grim, "Sitting-in for Disability Rights: The Section 504 Protests of the 1970s," National Museum of American History, Behring Center, *O Say Can You See?* (blog), July 8, 2015, https://americanhistory.si.edu/blog /sitting-disability-rights-section-504-protests-1970s.

CHAPTER 8: THE WHITE HOUSE

1. The following account of our trip to Washington and our experiences there, including direct quotes, are from D'Lil, *Becoming Real in 24 Days*, 140–65.

CHAPTER 9: THE RECKONING

1. Adrienne Phelps Coco, "Diseased, Maimed, Mutilated: Categorizations of Disability and an Ugly Law in Late Nineteenth-Century Chicago," *Journal of Social History* 44, no. 1 (Fall 2010): 23–37 https://www.jstor.org /stable/40802107.

2. Brian T. McMahon and Linda R. Shaw, *Enabling Lives: Biographies of Six Prominent Americans with Disabilities* (Boca Raton, FL: CRC Press, 2000), 78–79.

3. McMahon and Shaw, *Enabling Lives*, 79.

4. McMahon and Shaw, *Enabling Lives*, 79.

5. McMahon and Shaw, *Enabling Lives*, 80.

6. Arlene Mayerson, "The History of the Americans with Disabilities Act: A Movement Perspective," Disability Rights Education and Defense Fund, 1992, https://dredf.org/about-us/publications/the-history-of-the-ada.

7. "The Little Girl Who Crawled Up the Capitol Steps 25 Years Later: Jennifer Keelan and the ADA," *CP Daily Living*, July 24, 2015, http://cpdailyliving.com/the-little-girl-who-crawled-up-the-capitol-steps-25-years-later-jennifer-keelan-and-the-ada.

8. William Eaton, "Disabled Persons Rally, Crawl Up Capitol Steps: Congress: Scores Protest Delays in Passage of Rights Legislation. The Logjam in the House Is Expected to Break Soon," *Los Angeles Times*, March 13, 1990, https://www.latimes.com/archives/la-xpm-1990-03-13-mn-211-story.html.

CHAPTER 12: OUR STORY

1. Jeff Sessions, US Senate speech, May 2000.

2. Tom McCarthy, "All the President's Judges: How Trump Can Flip Courts at a Record-Setting Pace," *Guardian*, May 11, 2019, www.theguardian.com/law/2019/may/11/trump-judge-nominees-appointments-circut-court-flip.